# Heaven For Beginners

# Heaven For Beginners

## Recollections of a Southern Town

### Betsy Holloway

Persimmon Press

Orlando 1986

First Edition

Grateful acknowledgement is made for permission to quote from the following copyrighted works:

*This Was Home,* by Hope Summerell Chamberlain. (Chapel Hill: University of North Carolina Press, 1938) Copyright 1938, The University of North Carolina Press. Reprinted by permission of The University of North Carolina Press.

*The Story of Durham, City of the New South,* by William Kenneth Boyd. (Durham: Duke University Press, 1925) Copyright © 1925, Duke University Press. Reprinted by permission of Duke University Press.

*Good Morning, Miss Dove,* by Frances Gray Patton. (New York: Dodd, Mead & Company, 1954) Copyright © 1954 by Frances Gray Patton. Reprinted by permission of Frances Gray Patton and of Dodd, Mead & Company, Inc.

*Twenty-Eight Stories,* by Frances Gray Patton. (New York: Dodd, Mead & Company, 1969) Copyright © 1969 by Frances Gray Patton. Reprinted by permission of Frances Gray Patton and of Dodd, Mead & Company, Inc.

"PISTOL PACKIN' MAMA," by Al Dexter.
Copyright © 1942 Vogue Music. Copyright Renewed. (c/o The Welk Music Group, Santa Monica California, 90401). International Copyright Secured. All Rights Reserved. Used by Permission.

"THE ARMY AIR CORPS," by Major Robert M. Crawford.
Copyright © 1939, 1942, 1951 by Carl Fischer, Inc. New York. Copyrights Renewed. Used by Permission.

"DOWNTOWN," Words and Music by Tony Hatch.
© Copyright 1964 by Welbeck Music Ltd., London, England. Sole Selling Agent MCA Music, A Division of MCA Inc. New York, N.Y. for North, South and Central America. Used by Permission. All Rights Reserved.

Postcards and other illustrations are from the author's collection.

Library of Congress Catalog Card Number 86-60849

ISBN: 0-9616500-0-1

Persimmon Press, P.O. Box 536531,
Orlando, Florida 32853-6531.

# CONTENTS

# ILLUSTRATIONS

# Acknowledgements

A number of people have provided information and support that have enabled me to write this book. In Durham those persons include Gladys Bunting, Marie Crowder (of the Durham City Schools), Nancy Goodwin, Dr. William King (Duke Archives), Laurance and Eva Kirkland, Myra Markham, Laura Miller, Monte and Connie Moses, Dr. Ida Ruth Plymale (N.C. Museum of Life and Science), Lorraine Iseley Pridgen, Sandra Reaves, Vallie Robinson, and Vera Carr Twaddell. The staff members of the Durham Public Library have provided much help: Ann Berkeley in particular has been an inexhaustible and patient resource. Without the excellent memories and the interest of my mother, Ruth Gates McBroom, and my uncle, S. A. McBroom, the book in its present form couldn't have been written; and I'm grateful to them both.

Wyatt and Eugenia Dixon were kind enough to spend a morning sharing their knowledge with me. Mr. Dixon's and George Lougee's columns contain a gold mine of Durham's past; the town has been blessed in having these two writers preserve so much of what has gone before.

My special thanks to another talented and conscientious historian, Dr. Charles R. Sanders, who took time off from his own writing to offer information, advice, and encouragement.

Those outside of Durham who have helped include Margaret Chapman, JoAnn Dyer, Ann Eidson, Eli Evans, Betsy Hendrix, Cheri Henry, Nancy Hughes, Carole and Carolyn Langston, Katie Lowndes, Dr. David Lynn, and Peggy van den Berg. My husband and son have supplied answers to questions on a number of subjects. Staff members of the Orlando and Winter Park Public Libraries have patiently located several small needles in very large haystacks, and I greatly appreciate their help.

I'm especially grateful to several persons who have read portions of the book in manuscript: Laurance and Eva Kirkland, Carmel Mask, Ruth G. McBroom, and S. A. McBroom. Any errors that remain, of course, are mine alone.

This book had its beginnings four years ago in an *Orlando Sentinel* "Hometown" article: my thanks to Jeffrey Zaslow for writing that article, and to the *Sentinel* for publishing it. Hartwell Conklin, the *Sentinel*'s Public Relations Director and a transplanted Durhamite himself, was kind enough to send a copy of the article to the *Durham Morning Herald*; the *Herald*'s resulting . piece by John Adams aroused much favorable comment, and started me down this road.

To anyone who reads the book, the enormity of my debt to the *Durham Morning Herald*, the *Durham Sun*, and the earlier *Morning Herald* and *Durham Daily Sun*, will be obvious. Lewis Carroll wrote, "Come, tell me how you live...and what it is you do": I've tried to preserve a few aspects of how we lived, and what we did — the entertainment, the commercial offerings, the church activities, and especially the language and attitudes of times past. Much of what we did, and what we thought, resides in yesterday's newspapers, in ads and unsigned news articles that perfectly, and unconsciously, convey the unspoken assumptions of both writers and readers. To those faithful and anonymous chroniclers who recorded the life of their time better than they knew — and to my family, the Millers, Gateses, Bobbitts, McBrooms, and Holloways — this book is affectionately dedicated.

*Regarding history, I steadfastly believe*
*that it should be constructed as much as possible*
*out of chronicles of everyday life....*
*Who can tell what is of final importance,*
*and what is unessential?*

— *Hope Summerell Chamberlain*


*Home interprets heaven. Home is heaven for beginners.*

— *Charles Parkhurst*

# Heaven For Beginners

*P*rogress and enterprise is evident on every side,
and to think that where this proud and famous
little city now stands was, a few years ago,
almost a wilderness.
Is it not a grand illustration
of what enterprise and energy can do?

— *Hiram Paul, 1884*

# Prologue

That the city came to exist at all was almost happenstance. Once the region had been home to the Eno and Occoneechee Indians; early in the eighteenth century those tribes left to move northward, and some forty years later white settlers began to come to the area that would become eastern Orange County. By 1850 the region had a few well-defined settlements of which one, known as Pinhook, offered a variety of amusements that included liquor, sporting houses, and gambling; if a man were spoiling for a brawl, Pinhook was the place to go. A little further west stood a tavern kept by an enterprising trio, Ben Peeler and his sons Pet Titch-Eye and Red Wine: unwary travelers who stopped there in innocent search of refreshment were frequently robbed and murdered.

A few miles to the east, between Morrisburg and Hillsborough, stood Prattsburg, a small but thriving hamlet named for landowner William Pratt. During the early 1850's the North Carolina Railroad approached Pratt with a request to locate a station on his land. Reluctant to have a railway close to his store because he feared the noise would frighten his customers' horses, Pratt asked an exorbitant price for his property right-of-way. Word of the difficulty soon reached a young bachelor physician who lived in the countryside between Prattsburg and Pinhook; quick to seize an opportunity, Dr. Bartlett Durham promptly offered four acres of his own land for the station. The offer was gratefully accepted; and in honor of the donor, the station became Durhamville, then Durham's Station, and afterward simply Durham.

By the end of the Civil War the village had some two hundred inhabitants, together with a modest tobacco trade. As Generals

5

Johnston and Sherman negotiated terms of surrender a few miles away, Durham itself was declared neutral ground. There the men of the blue and the grey met to swap horses and tales, shoot at targets, run footraces, and generally enjoy themselves. About a hundred yards from the railway station stood John Ruffin Green's two-story frame factory, filled with bright leaf tobacco that was ready for shipment; during the armistice the building was sacked as soldiers gathered around campfires to — literally — smoke pipes of peace. After surrender terms had been completed, both armies provided themselves with generous supplies of Green's tobacco, and began the march toward home.

On their return the soldiers remembered the distinctive Spanish Flavored Durham Tobacco that had brightened the waning days of the long war, and soon orders for the tobacco began to pour into town. Imitators promptly rushed to market "Durham Tobacco" and "Spanish Flavored Tobacco," so that John Green began to seek a distinctive trademark. Over a breakfast of fried oysters a friend pointed out the bull's neck pictured on a jar of Colman's Mustard — manufactured in Durham, England — and suggested that Green adopt a bull as his trademark and name his product Bull Durham. Green followed the friend's advice, and soon an imposing picture of a bull adorned the front of his factory. Some years later, at the height of the brand's popularity, four crews of sign painters traveled the nation; and even one of the Pyramids boasted a likeness of the Bull. (In the course of the company's history several different signs were used, and at one point complaints from offended local residents caused the current symbol's impressive hinder parts to be revised into less prominence.) Green's business was purchased a few years later by W. T. Blackwell, whom a historian of that era would term the father of Durham, citing the "establishment and successful conduct of his tobacco manufacture" as well as his encouraging and sustaining the community in its growth from a straggling village into a busy, thriving town.

A few miles away, widower Washington Duke had returned to his war-scarred farm after serving in the Civil War — with distinction, though not without reluctance — to face the demands of providing for his children, Mary, Ben, and James ("Buck"). (Brodie, Washington Duke's son by an earlier marriage, was already nineteen and about to try a year of farming with an uncle.) Facing a bleak future with — as tradition has it — only a fifty-cent piece and two blind mules, Duke gathered together a small store of tobacco that had somehow escaped the attention of raiding soldiers; he flailed it, packed it into bags, charitably christened it "Pro Bono Publico," loaded his wagon, and with Ben and "Buck," aged ten and nine respectively, set out for eastern Carolina to peddle the new product. (They provided themselves with corn meal, sweet potatoes, and a side of bacon for their meals, and slept on the roadside at night.)

The Dukes sold and bartered their goods without difficulty, and at journey's end decided to continue with the manufacture and sale of tobacco, soon building a small factory for that purpose. The business prospered; by 1869 Brodie, whose enthusiasm for farming had faded with his small financial returns, had moved into Durham to begin his own tobacco firm, choosing "Semper Idem" and later "Duke of Durham" as his brands. (A colorful and oft-married individual in later life, Brodie would become one of Durham's strongest boosters, as well as an influential developer of real estate.) A few years later Ben, "Buck," and the senior Duke joined Brodie in Durham, and W. Duke, Sons and Company was established.

Sales increased steadily, but James B. Duke soon became dissatisfied with the company's failure to compete with the popular "Bull." Already, at twenty-five, the daring entrepreneur and business genius of the family, in 1881 he turned the firm's interest toward the manufacture of cigarettes (it was at that time that the community received its first Jewish residents, who moved from the North to take jobs making cigarettes by hand). A few years later the Duke firm adopted the newfangled Bonsack cigarette machine that when finally perfected could do the work of dozens of laborers: the machine's efficiency reduced the cost of cigarettes by more than one-half, while about the same time taxes were cut to one-third of their former rate. W. Duke, Sons and Company promptly cut its price fifty per cent, thus making its cigarettes the cheapest on the market. With the aid of imaginative advertising, much of which involved pictures of beautiful and seductive women, cigarettes quickly found widespread popularity, on which foundation James B. Duke would within a few years pen the Bull himself. Duke would also establish the American Tobacco Company, a conglomerate so vast and complex that when — twenty years later — the government ordered its dissolution, only the man who had created that empire had the ingenuity necessary to divide it.[1]

By 1880, Durham had begun to boom. A historian observes that it was a "high-living, hard-working, sporting town" where money and liquor flowed freely; Blackwell's race track was the finest in the state, and the best horses, carriages, and accessories were to be found in Durham. The town boasted at least one red light district (as a bow to propriety, however, the denizens were not allowed on the streets), and on one occasion a repentant mayor had himself arraigned and fined for drunkenness. On Christmas Eve the women and children of the town stayed safely in their homes while the men celebrated on Main Street with whiskey and fireworks. Despite the

---

[1]James B. Duke's bold and complicated business maneuvers frequently tried his father's patience as well as his nerves. Often quoted is the senior Duke's remark that there were three things he never could understand: "Ee-lec-tricity — the Holy Ghost — and my son Buck."

restraining presence of several young churches, it seemed Durham was carrying on the Pinhook tradition of being a "roaring old place."

Certain longings for respectability were coming to the fore, though, and streets that had originally borne such homely names as Shake Rag, Dog Trot, and Hen Peck Row acquired dignity in their new styles of McMannen, Pettigrew, and Dillard. Soon, too, the mayor's court discontinued its early custom of meeting under a tree in good weather, and moved indoors to conduct its affairs in more formal surroundings. A bank had been established, greatly alleviating the previous awkward necessity for brokers' canvassing the town for currency in order to meet the cash demands of large tobacco sales. As the town prospered and population grew, needs also increased for recording of deeds, filing of mortgages, and other governmental functions that could be accomplished only in Hillsborough, fifteen miles away; and soon a movement arose to establish Durham as the seat of its own county. In 1881, after much spirited and sometimes acrimonious legislative debate, a division was effected that created the new county from two others, Wake and Orange. Durham set out on her own path.

Soon the town's industry began to diversify. General Julian S. Carr,[2] who in 1871 had joined the Bull Durham firm as head of the mercantile and financial divisions (by 1883 he was president of the company), joined with several others to establish a cotton manufacturing firm: initially the mill's chief product was a cloth for use in the production of tobacco bags, but later it produced chambrays and ginghams as well. The Duke interests established a cotton mill likewise, choosing the site of old Pinhook for its location, and pragmatically naming the new firm Erwin Cotton Mill after its young manager.

[2]The "General" was an honorary title, bestowed by Confederate veterans in gratitude for Carr's many kindnesses. Carr had actually served as a private in the Confederate Army.

(Benjamin Duke reasoned sensibly that this choice of name would ensure that if the mill failed, the onus would be upon its manager, whereas if it prospered, its success would be to his glory.) Thirty years later the mill had expanded into four additional locations and was producing sheets and pillowcases, tickings, and canton flannel in addition to denims. The hosiery industry entered the picture around 1894, and textiles were soon to assume a place second only to tobacco in Durham's economy.

Rich the town was, with its fast horses and fine carriages, and with the grand houses of General Carr, the Dukes, and others to attest to its wealth; energetic and hardworking it was, filled with the excitement of tobacco sales, the hum and bustle of textile production; a place of opportunity it was, offering jobs to all those willing to work — but what of its Culture? In fact, very little. Durham was a brash, uncouth, tobacco-chewing upstart in the eyes of its Old South neighbors — aristocratic, historic Hillsborough; classical, ivory-towered Chapel Hill with its state university that was already nearly a century old; sophisticated, politically astute Raleigh, wise in the ways of governance. The reputation of being a "roaring old place" stubbornly clung; and when in 1888 the Baptists soberly looked around for a suitable location for their Female Seminary, Durham's offer of sixteen acres of land plus $50,000 (twice the amount bid by any other town) was rejected on the grounds that the town was "no fit place for young females." Durham was not amused.

But about that same time President John Crowell was making the decision to move his struggling Trinity College, then fifty years old, from rural Randolph County into a city. (Like many institutions of its day, Trinity had been established in the country in order to protect the morals of its students from urban temptation.) As the college flirted briefly with the notion of going to Raleigh, General Carr offered to donate for its use the fifty acres of Blackwell's racetrack and park on the western edge of town, while Washington Duke sweetened the bid with $85,000. This combination proved irresistible, and in 1892 Durham acquired Trinity College for its own. The school was to remain Trinity for thirty-two years longer, until James B. Duke's Endowment transformed it — changing its name, adding a splendid new campus, and laying a foundation for the university that exists today — with a magic wand that consisted of a golden, fragrant, carefully rolled Bright Leaf.

\* \* \* \* \*

As did Durham herself, this particular story begins in Orange County....

*Lord, with what care hast Thou begirt us round!*
*Parents first season us...*

— *George Herbert*

# CHAPTER 1
# Parents First

In the mid-eighteenth century North Carolina's Orange County had been large and powerful, with a border that extended north to the Virginia line. Hillsborough, the county seat, was a busy trading center as well as an important site for political activity throughout the Colonial period (the 1775 Provincial Congress convened there, along with several General Assemblies and the 1788 Constitutional Convention). At one time an attempt was even made to name Hillsborough the state capital, but this project was unsuccessful; and then during the years between 1779 and 1881 Orange County lost approximately ninety percent of its territory, including the rich industrial areas that became Alamance and Durham Counties. By 1900 Hillsborough's importance had faded into that of any small town with a glorious past, while ten miles away Chapel Hill remained a tiny, unprepossessing university village that may have boasted more dogs than either townspeople or students. Outside those two towns Orange County was almost entirely rural, a patchwork quilt of small farms whose owners were hard-working and independent as they had to be to wrest a living from that sometimes inhospitable Piedmont land.

It was soon after the turn of the century that my father was born into a family that had lived and farmed in Orange County for over a hundred and fifty years. His father, John Albert McBroom, was a farmer and a magistrate, a courtly and charming man who reared his brood with a firm hand, not sparing the rod when he thought discipline required it, and who at eighty peremptorily ordered a closefisted forty-year-old son to share his tobacco money with his wife. (The son obeyed posthaste.) My grandfather married three times: each of his first two wives died after bearing one child, but his third marriage, to the former Mattie Lee Bobbitt, proved both fruitful and long-lasting. An eighty-year-old photograph shows the couple with their first baby as well as my grandfather's two children from his earlier marriages: he and my grandmother are seated in front of their farmhouse with my Uncle Charlie, a shy, gawky teenager, standing behind them. My grandfather, a handsome, dark-haired, bearded man dressed in his Sunday suit, bowtie slightly awry, stares resolutely into the camera as he holds my Aunt Lurlie, a pretty, awed-looking child of three; my grandmother, an attractive young woman wearing her hair in a pompadour, holds Lula, her baby, and scowls darkly, furious with her husband for having given her only a few minutes' notice that they were to have their picture taken. This momentary discord notwithstanding, usually the marital skies were sunnier: fourteen children would be born of their union, of whom twelve — six boys and six girls — would live to adulthood. The second oldest of the twelve, my father, was christened Joseph Ira after Dr. Joseph Ira Coleman, the country doctor who had delivered him.

They lived the typical Piedmont farm life of the early twentieth century. Year round, my grandmother tended babies, sewed, mended, washed clothes in iron pots over a fire, kept house, and cooked three large meals each day. During late spring, summer, and early autumn my grandfather and the older children worked in the fields from dawn to dusk with the aid of plows, hoes, and mules; my grandmother worked alongside them, having first placed the baby in a box at the end of the row where the next child would stay to watch. They grew tobacco, the Golden Weed, for their cash crop, and sold it at the Durham market each year to buy occasional luxuries — peppermint candy, fresh oranges, a hoop of cheese — together with overalls, coffee, and the few other necessities that couldn't be produced on their farm. They grew vegetables — corn and tomatoes, okra and beans, squash and cabbage — to feed the ever-growing family, and in the summertime the older girls helped their mother with the churning, canning, and preserving. They raised hogs and chickens for meat; planted sugar cane for molasses; grew apples and pears for baking and drying; and kept a cow for milk. Church on Sunday; visits from neighbors; swimming in the creek; an occasional church supper or baseball game for entertainment.

During the late fall and winter, when farm chores were relatively light, the children attended the tiny New Bethel School nearby. Despite their work load at home, all of them continued their schooling through the eighth or ninth grade; a few even managed to finish all eleven grades and receive a high school diploma. Among those who dropped out in the ninth grade was my father, who stayed at home to farm for a few years before joining the slow but steady exodus of young people from farms into nearby towns: he was twenty-four when he left home to move to Durham, eighteen miles away and already a city of fifty thousand, in order to live with a cousin and begin work at Liggett and Myers's cigarette factory. His brother Sam came to Durham about the same time, taking a job as a bus and streetcar operator for the Durham Public Service Company (formerly Durham Traction Company, and later to become Duke Power Company); only a few months later, my father joined him. Both brothers would remain with the company for several decades — my father for forty years, my uncle for forty-five — until they retired.

Within a few months of their employment, the two brothers saw the end of the streetcar era in Durham. The last trolley was brought back to the barn on the Saturday evening of 25 January 1930, "Pop" Avent driving; beginning the next day, only buses were used. (A few buses had already been put into use before trolley service was discontinued.) Several days later the Durham Public Service Company ran newspaper ads announcing that "the streetcars in Durham have been replaced by new, swift and comfortable buses." The new system's capabilities were quickly tried by a heavy snowfall; but a few days afterward a *Herald* article proudly headlined the verdict: "Durham, With Complete Motorized System, Rides To Work While Trolley Cars In Other Cities Are Tied Up By Heavy Snows." Even during that period of abnormally heavy use and difficult road conditions, the buses proved a happy solution to the city's growing transportation needs. (The old streetcars were sold for use in Toledo.)

Bus service on most routes began at 5:30 a.m. Preferring to have his free time during the afternoons, my father always chose the early shift, so that throughout most of his working life he arose, dressed, breakfasted, and drove to work before dawn. By all accounts he was a conscientious, loyal employee who enjoyed bantering with his co-workers, and who in the evenings attended meetings of the company's social organization, the Doherty Men's Fraternity. (Local talent sometimes enlivened the Fraternity's dinners: one program included songs and dances by Eva and Doris Nachamson, two of the eight daughters of the hardworking and community-minded owners of United Dollar Store.)

Despite his shyness my father was a friendly man, always talking and joking with his passengers, who would remember him for years after his retirement; the elderly and infirm received his kindest care. A photograph taken when he was about thirty-five reveals a trim, erect young man dressed in his Durham Public Service uniform — navy blue wool gabardine with gold buttons — and walking with a long, healthy stride; his pleasant, serious expression shows only his quiet side, offering little hint of the cheerful, fun-loving man he became with his friends. To my knowledge he never raised his voice in anger to my mother; with me he lost his temper only once, though memorably, when as a toddler I slipped out of the yard to investigate a tree across the street. His own schooling limited, he would all his life remain mildly perplexed by a child who spent so much time silently absorbed in books, though he took pride in the A's I brought home on report cards. (He understood, too, how to stimulate my thirst for knowledge: each A earned me a quarter in hard cash.) Though his sentimental side was well known to my mother, I rarely glimpsed it; only after his death did I discover a tiny notebook that he'd owned as a youth. Inside the book, whose cover extolled the merits of F. W. Royster Fertilizers, he had painstakingly copied out seventy-five short verses of the sort popularly inscribed in autograph books of the time — "Cedar is green, so is pine; I'll be yours if you will be mine." "Roses are red, lilies are white; Being with you is my delight." Preserved along with his handwritten compilation of verses was the forty-year collection of birthday, anniversary, Easter, and Christmas cards that he'd given my mother — all with loving messages, all signed in his neat, small script, "Love, Mac."

His organizational bonds meant much to him. Soon after his marriage he had transferred his church membership to West Durham Methodist, where from then on he attended Sunday-School along with morning and evening services each week, served as an usher, and joined the other members of the Fred Thomas Bible Class for the long, cold evenings of selling Christmas trees. He treasured the Masonic affiliation that he, like his father, had acquired as a young man; and he studied hard to memorize the long graveside rite that he would perform for two dozen of his fellow Masons, sometimes holding back tears for a friend while — letter-perfect — he recited traditional, cadenced words of victory over death. When he was in his forties he became a member of Durham's Sudan Temple, and then he proudly wore his red fez for ceremonial occasions (our Plymouth's rear windshield sported a tiny fez of its own), contributed to the Crippled Children's Hospital, and spent some of his happiest hours attending Shrine gatherings with his friends.

His favorite hymn was "This Is My Father's World"; his passion, the out-of-doors. He spent his weekday afternoons keeping our yard weeded, trimmed, and in bloom; he enjoyed fishing when he had a chance to go; but above all else he loved hunting quail. Always we owned a pair of hunting dogs, a short-haired pointer and a silky, long-haired setter; and each September my father re-enacted his annual ritual of preparation — buying a case of shotgun shells, checking the gun that he would have spent half a day cleaning at the end of the previous season, unhurriedly inspecting the condition of his high boots and heavy socks. When October's cool weather arrived he began working with his dogs, taking them out into the fields each day for exercise. He looked forward eagerly to hunting on Thanksgiving, the first day of quail season, though he really preferred other, quieter days when fewer huntsmen crowded the countryside. After Thanksgiving he hunted every day until the season ended: on arriving home from work each afternoon he quickly changed into yellowish-brown hunting clothes and drove out into the country to tramp through fields until dark; usually he went alone, but if one of his hunting buddies could go, he welcomed the company. A scrupulous sportsman, he carefully observed the game limits; and he left off hunting on Sundays and after each snowfall. He prized his dogs: he trained them patiently, photographed them in the field, and cared for them lovingly, grieving over their sufferings when one fractured a leg or was bitten by a snake.

# PARENTS FIRST

My father was already in his fifties when he was given, by a former fireman who'd won the Irish Sweepstakes some twenty years before, a finely-wrought old German shotgun; it became his proudest possession, a treasured symbol of the sport he loved. But only a few years later his cheerful disposition became subdued, and he began to slow and stumble; and soon doctors told us he was experiencing the early effects of a rapid physical deterioration for which there would be no cure. His friends came by faithfully to take him hunting with them long after he had given up driving; but finally the day came when he put away his cherished shotgun for the last time, sold his dogs, and hunted no more.

He lived a few years longer, slowly fading into a silent shadow of the man he once had been; his quiet death, when it came, seemed only a footnote to what had happened long before. At his funeral we sang "This Is My Father's World"; his Masonic brothers spoke their farewells in a country churchyard, not far from the fields he'd loved. In the distance a quail sang, perhaps calling him home.

* * * * *

Likewise born into an old Orange County farm family, my mother was the adored only child of parents who had married just a year before her birth. My grandmother, Kittie Miller, had been one of nine children of Charlie Rountree Miller, a farmer, Civil War veteran, government still operator, and landowner who, it was rumored, could at one time ride his horse the ten miles to Hillsborough without leaving his own land. For several years after her brothers and sisters had married and left home Kittie had remained, caring first for her invalid sister Emma and then for her father during his last illness; a few years after his death, just when she thought herself comfortably settled into a life of spinster aunthood, neighboring storekeeper Stephen Gates's youngest son came calling, and her expectations under-

went a sea-change. Bob Gates, whose sister Minnie was married
to Kittie's brother Bob, was mustached and handsome, with
a slightly rakish appearance resulting from a misshapen left
eyelid; possessed of little education, he was said to have been
"spoiled rotten" by his grandmother during the years she had
cared for him after his mother's early death. Nevertheless, when
he asked Kittie to marry him, she agreed. She was then thirty-
nine and he twenty-four; and on hearing news of the betrothal,
staid Caldwell Community erupted in indignation: "What kind
of CHILDREN will they have?" shrilled one outraged relative.
But Kittie, whose gaze was clear and determined and whose
mind was her own, had decided that after her years of caring
for others it was time to shape a life for herself. She was a
landholder, the owner of a farm that her father had given her
as he had done for each of his other children; and though her
tall, slim figure, dark hair, and serene eyes were undeniably
attractive, doubtless her property also held some interest for
her suitor, who owned no land of his own. In any case they
married, and despite the age difference and my grandfather's
fiery temper the union proved stable: it would be severed only
by my grandmother's death thirty years later.

During her childhood my mother lived with her parents on
their farm, where she helped plant tobacco and repair fences,
slid down haystacks with friends, made molasses cookies with
her mother, and visited cousins and neighbors, sometimes for
a week at the time. Animals helped to fill her life: an assortment
of cats vied for her attention, and her collie Shep followed her
devotedly all over the farm and up to Little River Church half
a mile away. Life continued peacefully and predictably until
she was twelve, when her parents decided that she would
benefit from more schooling than was available at the two-room
Caldwell School that, like New Bethel and most other rural
schools, stayed open for only four months of the year. That
fall, with some apprehension and a few quiet tears, she packed

22

up her three gingham "aprons" for school, her long black stockings, and her Sunday dress, to go and live in town.

In that year, 1917, Durham (including the unincorporated villages of East Durham and West Durham) had a population of 33,000; the town boasted forty-six churches, a public library, and several clubs, one of them the Durham Country Club. The

*Postcard view of Durham's Country Club, ca. 1916.*

public school system included six schools for white children, three for black. The town's nine banks included the Morris Plan Bank and one "colored" bank; the Fidelity Bank advertised resources of $3,000,000 and paid four percent interest on time deposits. Roads were macadamized or sand-clay (chiefly the latter); and a large number of area residents had electric lighting in their homes. And in West Durham, the old open dry closets were being replaced by septic tanks, in the view of area residents a welcome sanitary improvement.

The town's industries were booming. Each day Erwin Cotton

Mills used nearly 100 bales of cotton to produce wide sheeting, pillowcases, and linens; the Golden Belt plant, the largest cotton bag mill in the world, produced 2,000,000 assorted bags; Durham Hosiery Mills, the largest hosiery concern in the world, produced 342,000 "Durable Durham" brand socks and hose. And Durham manufacturers and exporters purchased 70,000,000 pounds of tobacco each year, most of it used to produce Bull Durham and Duke's Mixture tobaccos, along with several brands of cigarettes.

DURHAM, N. C.   Duke's Factory.

*Postcard view of Duke's Factory, ca. 1910.*

Downtown Durham was bustling and busy. Close to Five Points stood Kronheimer's, one of the town's several excellent department stores, wherein a lady might purchase the finest of china, linen, and wearing apparel — striped sport skirting taffetas, middy blouses, crepe de chines, gauze lisle or silk hose, La Grecque corsets; double-bed-size crepe or seersucker counterpanes ($1.50); "Jap hand-painted China," unsurpassed in quality. At the corner of Main and Mangum, Haywood & Boone (The Drug and Seed Store Where Quality Counts) offered

*Postcard view of Bull Factory, ca. 1910.*

maple fudge, log cabin, and silver sundaes for ten and fifteen cents, as well as Cow-Ease to rid cows and horses of flies, and Corona Dry to kill potato bugs. Just a few doors west, Durham Book and Stationery offered books, office supplies, writing paper, and everything for school, from booksacks to drinking cups; in the front of the store, under large ceiling fans, a soda fountain provided a popular gathering place for the young set to laugh, flirt, and drink ice cream sodas (or Orange Jooj, Coca-Cola's new fruit drink). Across the street stood Baldwin's, several years resident in the city, offering millinery, muslin underwear, sheets and counterpanes, waistings and skirtings.

Ellis-Stone, already thirty years old and a new resident of the location it would keep for the next twenty years, offered shantung-silk suits and Betty Wales linen dresses together with An Endless Display Of Pure White Silks, Crepes, And Chiffons For The Bride; next door, Woolworth's had just settled into its own new location for what would prove to be a very long stay indeed. Jones & Frasier, Jewelers and Optometrists, were selling

25

*Two early views of Main Street.*

"Wedding Rings That Bind" in their new space next to the recently-built First National Bank Building. Diagonally across from the bank stood the post office, a graceful Beaux Arts building whose front sidewalk was for years favored by Trinity

College's, and then Duke's, fraternities as a gratifyingly visible spot to have hapless pledges spend the day fishing in a bucket of water, or else handing out sheets of toilet paper to surprised women passersby.

*Postcard view of post office, ca. 1908.*
*(To the left, the Trust Building; to the right, the Academy of Music.)*

At the corner of Main and Church Streets, Victor Kaplan was offering for sale, at a fraction of value, the entire stock of Mrs. A. E. Shockley, one of East Durham's most popular milliners. On East Main Street Frank Green and Miss Lillie May Poteat, booksellers and stationers, provided Everything For The Office, while on Corcoran Street — opposite the post office — Christian & Harward, The Happy Home-makers, offered Everything in Home Furnishings. Around the corner, on Parrish Street, stood the offices of North Carolina Mutual and Provident Association, The Greatest Negro Insurance Company In The World, advertising gross assets of $270,000. Joseph S. Hall and George V. Wynne maintained a funeral parlor and livery establishment on Morris Street, just off Five Points. On Chapel Hill Street, Mallie

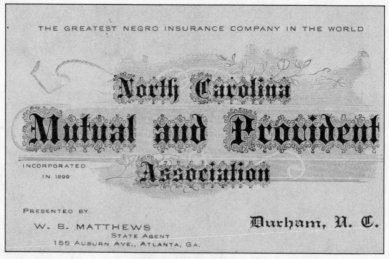

*Business card, ca. 1912.*

*Postcard view of North Carolina Mutual and
Provident Association office, ca. 1912.*

Paschall's Durham Star Bakery advertised its Health Bread as
"the best six cent loaf you can buy." And across from the post
office, the stately, newly-built, Italianate Geer Building —

mindful of the disastrous fire three years before that had destroyed that site's previous occupant — offered Modern, Fireproof Offices For Rent. (Already occupying a fourth-floor studio was Mrs. Florence Eakes, who sold La Carmille and Bien Jolie corsets to ladies of discernment.)

*View of Main Street, ca. 1908.*
*Buildings in left foreground were destroyed in 1914 fire.*

Further east on Main Street, a flurry of building had recently taken place. The splendid new First Presbyterian Church had risen in Gothic Revival glory of red brick and limestone, replacing a simpler and smaller brick structure on the same site. Across the street stood the four-year-old Malbourne Hotel, solidly constructed of red brick and secure in its position as Durham's premier hostelry.[1] (General Julian S. Carr's grand seventy-room Queen Anne hotel, the towered and turreted

---

[1] A post card mailed only a few weeks after the hotel's opening read, "The Hotel Malbourne where I am stopping is the only building I ever saw that was advertised to be fireproof that looked like it was. Has steel doors between sections of it."

Carrolina, had burned six years before the Malbourne was built.) Across Main Street the YMCA, now nine years old, was elder resident in the immediate area; a few steps away, next to the Hotel Lochmoor, the County's government offices had recently occupied the brand new, gleaming white limestone building that had succeeded the old brick courthouse, where the town's only two hangings had taken place. And next door to the Malbourne, only a few days after the courthouse opening, one of Durham's most glamorous evenings thus far had opened a new theater — the Orpheum.

*Postcard view of old First Presbyterian Church, ca. 1909.*

The opening took place on the evening of 28 November 1916: the first-night crowd, filled with enthusiasm and eager to be pleased, found that everything about the evening delighted them. Guy Johnson, performing as "Jake," the popular blackface comedian, had presented *The Dolly Dimple Girls*, a musical comedy and vaudeville revue that starred Miss Elsie Johnson; Louise Wright performed as the girl comedian, and

*Postcard view of Carrolina Hotel, ca. 1906.*

*Postcard view of YMCA, ca. 1915.*

Grace Hutchison sang the blues. Weist and Meyers, "two singing lads and a piano," made an immediate hit with the audience, which demanded several encores. (Two days previous

*Postcard view of Hotel Malbourne and Orpheum Theatre, ca. 1917.*

to the opening, the theater owners' *Morning Herald* ad had assured Durhamites that "the Orpheum will offer only clean, wholesome amusement with nothing to offend the most refined taste of the amusement seeker...it will be a theater that ladies, gentlemen and children will find pleasure in attending.") Opening night had seen the auditorium packed to capacity; the building's appointments, as the *Herald* later reported, were "first-class and up-to-date in every particular," with a marble and tile lobby, auditorium decorated in pleasing shades of green and gold, and chandeliers of hammered antique brass and cathedral glass in soft amber. The seats were finished in a waxed French grey; the stage was equipped with a splendid array of scenery, and illuminated by hundreds of footlights. Orchestra seats cost twenty cents, balcony seats a dime.

Entertainment was in fact plentiful and varied. The Academy of Music, just behind the post office, offered minstrels and other stage attractions as well as a few motion pictures: D. W. Griffith's *Birth of a Nation* had played to packed houses the year before, and the 1917 season opened with Harry Stubbs starring in *Nothing But The Truth* ("A bombshell of laughter...a cyclone of fun"). (A few years later, in 1921, the Academy would provide the setting for a historic meeting: during rehearsals for the annual Elks' Club minstrel, a Chicago production company sent an aspiring director, a young man of twenty, to work with an older, experienced professional. From this meeting of Freeman Gosden and Charles Correll came the long-lasting partnership that would create the most successful radio show of the 1930's, *Amos 'n' Andy*.)

*Postcard view of Academy of Music, ca. 1908.*

Southwest of town, Lakewood Park offered every amusement imaginable from swimming to roller skating, drama to dancing. (Those requiring instruction in the latter could learn Modern Dances of New York with Mr. and Mrs. H. L. Martin on Monday, Wednesday, and Friday evenings in the ballroom of the Hotel Lochmoor, Victrola Music Courtesy Of The Corley Company.) At the Paris Theatre one could watch George M. Cohan make his screen debut in *Broadway Jones,* or else weep

Hotel Lochmoor, Durham, N. C.

*Postcard view of Hotel Lochmoor, ca. 1915.*

over the performance of Pauline Frederick, The Season's Greatest Emotional Actress, in *Her Better Self;* admirers of Charlie Chaplin could see *Easy Street* or *Charlie's Hard Luck* at the Strand. Durham's younger citizens weren't forgotten either: in September the *Morning Herald* reported that during the summer eight thousand children had enjoyed good supervision, fresh air, sunshine, and exercise at the city's playgrounds (three for white, one for colored).

Durham took pride in its music. The DeBolle Music Studio offered violin, piano, theory, ensemble class, and a students' orchestra, while the Durham School of Music, under the

34

While in Durham if You Wish to See a

# GENUINE MOTION PICTURE

Production, Visit the

# PARIS, BROADWAY

OR

# STRAND THEATRES

## Craver Amusement Enterprises

**CONTINUAL SERVICE 11 A.M. TO 11 P.M.**

*Advertisement in Trinity College annual, 1920.*

direction of Mrs. A. R. Wynn and Miss Daisy Robbins, offered studies in Piano, Voice, Culture and Theoretical Work In All Its Branches. Miss Tillett's Private School offered individual attention and limited its number of pupils to twenty. Largest of all the music schools was the two-story, Italianate Southern Conservatory of Music at Main and Duke Streets, established in 1898 by Gilmore Ward Bryant at the request of Benjamin Duke. Both boarding and day pupils studied at the Conservatory, which maintained its own orchestra and presented frequent student recitals, together with well-known artists in concert. (On a less exalted level, a person suffering simultaneous gastronomic and musical cravings could satisfy both thirsts at the Main Street Pharmacy, which offered in its soda fountain a Violano Virtuoso — an automatic violin and player piano combination — for its customers' diversion.)

Other educational institutions were thriving as well. The National Religious Training School and Chautauqua, originally

*Postcard view of Southern Conservatory of Music, ca. 1910.*

established in 1909 to train black ministers and other religious workers, had recently been re-christened the National Training School, in keeping with the school's new objective of offering

*Postcard view of National Religious Training School and Chautauqua, ca. 1911.*

standard academic courses. On the opposite side of town stood Trinity College, now twenty-five years resident in the city. Having arrived in 1892 with its belongings in one boxcar, Trinity now boasted an attractive campus of 102 acres, twenty-four buildings, and holdings valued at $3,000,000; the school had had 805 students, and sixty-four teachers and officers, during the preceding year. The graduating seniors of the Class of 1917 heard an address on "The Creed of Jesus," delivered by Dr. James S. Montgomery of Calvary Methodist Church in Washington, D.C. During that summer the College's vegetable garden yielded an unusually bountiful crop, the produce from which was canned to be sold to the college boarding houses. (The College used its mules for much of the work, and kept the project's expenses low by assigning employees to do most of the gardening.)

*Postcard view of Trinity College gates, ca. 1908.*
*In the background stands the Washington Duke Building. (The gates were dismantled around 1914.)*

Canning clubs were in fact springing up all over town, for war was in the air. Secretary of the Navy Josephus Daniels came

*Trinity College Library, ca. 1912.*

*Trinity College campus, ca. 1906.*
*The Mary Duke Building, a dormitory, stands on the left; on the right is Craven Memorial Hall, behind which stands the Library.*

to Durham to speak to citizens about the conflict, and the city exceeded its quota of Liberty Loan bonds through the patriotism of Erwin Mills's W. A. Erwin, who subscribed to $250,000 in bonds. Miss Katie L. Johnson, Portrait Photographer, offered special rates on photographs of "new soldier boys in uniform," while along with school supplies and sodas, Durham Book and Stationery provided free of charge "a gold-stamped name on any Bible or Testament purchased for a soldier boy." And Lakewood Park cheerfully advised its patrons, "Prepare yourself for war by practicing at the Shooting Gallery."

In a two-story white frame house on Watts Street, on the northern outskirts of Durham, lived Uncle Sam and Aunt Jodie Miller and their six children, and it was with them my mother stayed. Her initial homesickness never entirely disappeared; but in September she settled into West Durham School, joining her cousins and her young half-aunt, Annie Gates, for the four-mile walk over dirt roads to and from school — walks enlivened by frequent stops by Wright's Grocery, across from the school, to buy dill pickles that would spice up homemade lunches of ham biscuits and sweet potato applejacks. (Within a few days of enrolling in West Durham, my mother was dismayed to find that her studies at Caldwell had prepared her insufficiently for her current level, so that she would have to repeat her last grade.)

In her free moments she could visit her Uncle Sam's busy grocery and feed store on North Road (later Club Boulevard), a block from his house; within a few weeks, having overcome her initial awe of the big house with indoor plumbing and electric lights, she had adjusted peaceably to the bustle and excitement of life in a large family. Each Wednesday she and her cousin Evelyn traveled downtown by streetcar to a frame building on Chapel Hill Street, close to the Academy of Music, to study piano with petite, elderly Miss Mary Holeman; on Saturdays the two girls ironed twenty-five white shirts for the males of the family; each night one of the two resignedly climbed out of bed to take a glass of water to young Wendell, the baby. Occasionally the whole family went downtown to take in such special events as the Twenty-Mule Borax Team parade. Once in a while my mother went home to the farm for a weekend reunion with her parents, who then put her on the Sunday evening train from Rougemont to return to the Union Station in Durham. Two years after their daughter had begun school in town, Bob and Kittie Gates rented out their farm in Orange County and moved to Durham; within a few months they had built a good-sized frame house on the northwest corner of North Road and Buchanan, facing open farmland and woods. As soon as they'd moved in, my mother, then a young teenager, happily joined them.

At school she shone in algebra and received awards for perfect attendance; though she was quiet and reserved, her senior description noted approvingly that she was "a friend worth while, regular and punctual and always to be depended upon." (Sumter "Zip" Brawley was voted the class's most mischievous member; Margaret "Pig" Dennis was Class Beauty; Boyd Brogden, Best Boy Athlete, was "one of Nature's specimens of physical beauty and grace." Eunice "Red" Smith was said to possess "that quality so rare among the fair sex — the power to talk little and think much.") The Class Prophecy affirmed,

> You know how queer Ruth Gates, Gertrude Limer, and Lottie McCoursley were about the proper sphere for women being in the home. They aspired to nothing better than a cozy home and contentment with what they had. They each met a man who was looking for just such a girl and the rest of the story need not be told in detail....I believe Ruth and Lottie are the happiest ones of the class.

The class chose as its motto, "Be as valuable as gold, and as rich in deeds as purple"; as its flower, the Dorothy Perkins Rose.

Three weeks before the class's graduation came May Day

exercises. Grassy, shaded Erwin Park provided a sylvan setting for the ceremony that crowned Margaret Teague as Queen, Eleanor Boing her Maid of Honor. Dances, including Maypole dances, were presented by students from all grades, who were arrayed in gay, colorful costumes for the celebration. The eighth grade danced to "I'm Forever Blowing Bubbles," while the first-graders presented a "Doll Dance"; the world was young, and Joy ruled the day.

Commencement exercises for West Durham's thirty-four graduating seniors, Class of 1925, took place in crowded, hot Erwin Auditorium on the evening of June 1: amid the gentle whirring of hand-held cardboard fans, a boys' quartet sang "Lassie O' Mine"; the girls' chorus sang "My Sunshine"; and on walking up to the stage to accept her diploma, each young woman graduate received baskets of flowers from her family and friends. The baccalaureate service had taken place the preceding evening at St. Philip's Episcopal Church, where the Reverend S. S. Bost had preached a sermon that next day's *Herald* sagely disclosed was "one in which profound thought was shown and excellent advice given." (In the recitation and declamation contest a few evenings before, Ruby Johns had recited "The Highwayman," Willie Culbreth had declaimed "Motherhood," and the Primary Grades had enacted "Making the Rainbow," which the printed program had helpfully summarized: "The Sunshine and Moondrops have a quarrel. The Flowers settle the dispute.")

September of the year following found my mother enrolled in a year's business course at the brand new Durham High School, joining Cosmo Cox and some two dozen others in studying commercial law with the city schools' business manager Marion Fowler, typing with the capable and conscientious Miss Ethel Solloway. As the holidays approached, Kronheimer's advertised, "We want the services of four bright salesladies until Christmas"; on the following day my mother answered the ad and was hired. Any young woman would have enjoyed Kronheimer's, with its snowy linens and colored silk umbrellas, silk-shaded piano lamps and sparkling crystal, silver mesh evening bags and daintily embroidered silk and batiste underwear; my mother loved the store, but her job plunged her unceremoniously into the mysteries of the pneumatic tube system, which at first nearly vanquished her. After surviving her initial plunge into the world of commerce, she returned to finish her business course; soon afterward she accepted an office position at Watts Hospital, where she would remain for the next ten years.

Watts Hospital, one of Durham's more noteworthy philanthropies, owed its existence to one of the city's best-known businessmen, George Washington Watts. Watts had moved to Durham from Baltimore in 1878, as a young man of twenty-seven, to join the tobacco firm of W. Duke, Sons and Company (Watts's father had provided the $14,000 that enabled him to purchase a one-fifth interest in the firm). Possessed of business acumen and community spirit, the new arrival prospered so quickly that six years later a local chronicler was already referring to him as "one of our most worthy and enterprising business men." In 1904 Watts founded the Home Savings Bank and then the Durham Loan and Trust Company; soon afterwards he spearheaded a successful fund drive to create a YMCA. The new First Presbyterian Church building was constructed in large part through his generosity; and a few years after Watts's death, historian William Kenneth Boyd wrote admiringly, "Of his riches he gave freely during his life, and his will revealed a bequest to the church of $150,000."

Watts Hospital began in 1895 on the northeast corner of West Main and Buchanan Boulevard, in a group of four cottage-style frame buildings that Watts donated to the city. In his dedicatory address at Stokes Hall on 21 February, Watts remarked on the warmth and hospitality that he, his wife and child had encountered since their move to Durham seventeen years before, observing, "What success we have achieved has been in your midst." He continued,

> It has been my desire for several years to show my appreciation of your fellowship and kindness, and to do so in such a manner as would benefit your people, and glorify the name of the Master, who has placed in my hands means with which to honor Him, and the responsibility as one of His stewards.

He had been a hospital patient some three years earlier, Watts explained, and then for the first time he had become aware of the value of services provided by trained nurses. Since that time he had devoted his attention and study to hospital work, subsequently concluding that such an institution would prove of great benefit to the citizens of Durham. Trinity College's President Kilgo responded gratefully and emotionally,

> It is appropriate to name an institution for its founder. This is the Watts Hospital, because you have put into it your ideas. It is your faith in men, your thoughts of the suffering. No doubt you have seen and heard the cries of pain. This is your response. I thank God, sir, that you have not only heard but answered. So I say you have told us more about yourself than we knew before.

Watts provided the $30,000 necessary to build the four hospital buildings, together with an endowment of $20,000. Of the twenty-two beds, all but four were free.

In 1895 the prevailing view of hospitals was morbid indeed: rather than places of healing, they were houses of death whose very presence was an intimation of mortality, and whose residents were mournfully expected to perish within a short time, if not immediately. In such a climate the new institution was at best a venture full of risk. But the town council voted it a monthly stipend of $100 that was soon increased to $200; a Hospital Aid Association was organized within the year; and

DURHAM, N. C    Watts Hospital.

*Postcard view of the first Watts Hospital, ca. 1908.*

various special events such as concerts and baseball games, some of them organized by local physicians, benefited the institution as well. Use of the hospital was at first discouragingly slight; but as physicians and former patients began to praise the institution, admissions gradually increased until less than fifteen years after its inception the hospital had outgrown its facilities. Thereupon George Watts selected a twenty-five acre site in the countryside northwest of town, and had constructed there an entirely new hospital, stuccoed Spanish Mission in style, and attractively designed with sun porches, large windows, and ventilating towers in order to provide patients with generous amounts of sunshine and fresh air. The new complex of six buildings, suitably equipped, cost $535,000; in addition Watts donated $300,000 in securities as permanent endowment. On presenting the hospital to Durham and its citizens on 2 December 1909, Watts expressed his hopes for the new institution:

May it ever be conducted in the true Christian or Christ-like spirit,

44

where all distinctions of class or creed fade away in the one universal desire to bind up the wounds, to relieve the pains, and strengthen the courage of our common humanity.

With its various additions and improvements, Watts Hospital would minister to the ill for nearly seventy years.

*Postcard view of the second Watts Hospital, ca. 1910.*

When my mother began work there, the hospital was only eighteen years old. Beds on the open wards for twelve cost two dollars per day; semi-private rooms were three dollars; and private rooms ranged from four to ten dollars (the noisier rooms, next to the diet kitchen and the elevators, cost four dollars; the quiet corner rooms with bath cost ten). Each morning the hospital superintendent and the superintendent of nurses made rounds of the entire hospital; each night Sam Lindsay covered the switchboard, entered and discharged patients on the hospital register, compiled reports, admitted emergencies, and dealt capably with the occasional inebriate who wandered through the front door that was never locked. (He also called the night supervisor to unlock the door of the Nurses' Home for those student nurses who were taking their monthly 11 p.m. evening out.)

On Lindsay's monthly night off his shift fell the lot of one of the daytime employees, my mother and the other five young women who worked in the office under the direction of tall, spare, exacting Miss Lottie Eure. In those days of simple hospital procedures they did everything: admitted patients (occasionally wondering whether the slow, crochety elevator could possibly convey an expectant mother upstairs before her baby arrived); operated the switchboard; made up the hospital's deposit and took it to the bank; prepared the handwritten bills to be taken around to patients who were being discharged; and paid the hospital accounts, always waiting until creditors pressed for payment, for the hospital was perpetually short of funds. (On occasion they also supplied information to young, harried-looking Duke fraternity pledges as to the number of windows in the hospital.)

Despite the professional formality that reigned — office staff and nurses stood respectfully when a physician entered the room, and addressed each other by their titles and last names — Watts's atmosphere was friendly and closeknit: employees rejoiced in the young nursing students' pride on being "capped"; a nurses' choir sang carols on each ward at Christmastime; the kitchen staff made ice cream that was everyone's favorite. A student nurse in straitened circumstances sometimes found herself enriched by a quiet gift of a few hard-earned dollars from an employee. When my parents built their house one of the hospital's board members supplied plants from his greenhouses, at a fraction of value, to landscape their yard; on entering the hospital's obstetrical unit a few years later, my mother was attended by nearly every physician on the staff.

When Duke University opened its hospital in 1930 Watts employees expected sure and certain ruin for their institution;

but from the start the University facility was considered suspiciously "experimental," and most Durhamites continued to patronize Watts. When times became hard soon thereafter, Duke and Watts joined forces to organize the Hospital Care Association, a private insurance plan that later would become Blue Cross-Blue Shield of North Carolina; at the urging of their employers, the hospital's own employees were among the first to buy such protection. Aided by insurance that helped to pay for treatment costs, patients continued to use the facility; and the hospital endured.

My mother was twenty-two when she began work at Watts; her photographs from that time show a dark-haired, blue-eyed, slender young woman whose expression is at once serenely happy and somewhat shy. She liked doing her meticulous record-keeping in the hospital's atmosphere of helping and healing; and she cherished her associations with physicians, co-workers, and nurses, some of whom would become lifelong friends. On Sunday afternoons she joined a group of eight or nine other young people who gathered to walk a few blocks south to what had been Trinity College but was now to be the Woman's College of the newly-established Duke University, or to the rock quarry or the spring a few hundred yards from my grandparents' house, or to one of the downtown soda fountains for ice cream or a cherry smash. Sometimes they spent the afternoon taking photographs with their square black Kodaks; other days two or three of them went out to ride in the Ford coupe that my grandfather (who never learned to read or write) had given my mother shortly before her high school graduation as a token of his pride in her accomplishment. (By that time, the late 1920's, a number of Durham's streets had been macadamized, providing a respite from dirt and mud; street signs and stop lights, though, remained rare.) Once they visited the new Washington Duke Hotel, a splendid yellow brick structure that had been built — by public subscription — behind the post office, on the site of the old Academy of Music;[1] one memorable Sunday several friends drove to Roxboro for a picnic at serene, beautiful Loch Lilly, where canoers paddled lazily, and water lilies drifted gently on the lake's surface. My mother

*Postcard view of the Washington Duke Hotel, ca. 1926.*

[1] A sumptuous Chamber of Commerce booklet published in 1926 extolled the new hotel as follows: "The spirit of Durham's progress is exemplified by the magnificent hotel erected here recently. This new hotel has three hundred bedrooms, each with bath, and it is richly furnished throughout. It has dining facilities capable of seating eleven hundred people at a meal, an excellent ballroom, and a large hall for luncheons, banquets, and conventions." The 1928 City Directory spoke of "Durham's no less than wonderful hotel...the largest and most magnificent in the State...."

was eighteen before she had her first date, and up until her marriage eleven years later her parents remained the authorities in her life, exercising considerable influence on where she went and what she did; happily, though, her friends Lois Overton, Bertha Almond, and the Guthrie sisters, all older than she, lived close by, so that — when partisans were needed — they could intervene on her behalf. At fifteen years her senior, Bertha was considered a particularly stable influence in whose company my mother was allowed to go anywhere without question. For these young people, funds were scarce and luxuries few; but pleasures were many.

Two years after my mother had begun work at the hospital, the Depression began. As times became bleak Durham citizens formed a Taxpayers League whose purpose was "to reduce unnecessary and excessive expenditure of public funds in the city and county, and reduce the tax rate to the lowest minimum without destroying the efficiency of government." Adopting the strong measures deemed necessary to provide relief to taxpayers, the determined League slashed salaries of city and county employees (including the salaries of the judge and prosecuting attorney of Recorder's Court), terminated employees whose jobs were adjudged to be superfluous, and suspended activities of the city's recreation department. Hard times had set in.

In the face of widespread unemployment together with salary cuts in both public and private sectors, my mother was fortunate enough to keep her job throughout the worst years of the Depression, dependably earning her fifteen dollars per week and relishing the freedom of having a Saturday afternoon and Sunday off each month. It was providential for their family that her job lasted, for her father lost his entire bank savings and had no cash reserves for three years; during that time my mother provided much of the family's support, buying groceries as well as paying city and county taxes on their home. But in back of their house my grandparents kept a large garden that produced the vegetables they needed for the table plus a few to sell; and their cow supplied milk and butter for use at home as well as extra buttermilk that my grandmother could sell for five cents a quart (surplus butter, when she had it, brought a quarter a pound). With negligible medical and automobile expenses, and my mother's having one or two meals each day at the hospital, their family was affected only lightly by the decade that brought suffering to so many others. And even when money was scarcest, my grandmother had her beloved flower garden, a riot of color with its yellow zinnias and red petunias, lavender phlox and marigolds, red and white sweet peas, imperious red cannas, and lush, fragrant pink peonies.

Two boy friends had preceded my father in my mother's affections, but Ira had grown up just a few miles from her parents' farm and their families knew each other; and one evening as the two sat in my grandparents' front porch swing, he proposed, and she accepted. They were married quietly at home by retired Methodist minister D. N. Caviness, who in his younger years had served in the Caldwell Community where he had known both the Gateses and the Millers, and who only two years later would conduct my grandmother's funeral, remarking on her faithfulness in caring for her invalid sister. A few close friends attended the marriage ceremony, one of them Watts graduate Mary Lena Duke, who would soon become Superintendent of the new Tuberculosis Sanatarium in Raleigh. My parents took four days away from their jobs to honeymoon in Roanoke and Washington, D.C., traveling in my mother's small coupe since my father owned no car. After living in rented rooms for a few months they moved back to live with my grandparents; but already they were looking at houses under construction and studying plans in magazines, and less than two years later they would have a home of their own.

*I have come back again to where I belong;*
*not an enchanted place, but the walls are strong.*

*— Dorothy H. Rath*

## CHAPTER 2
# The Walls Were Strong

North of Main Street, beginning at the Coca-Cola Bottling Plant and running alongside the eastern border of the stone wall enclosing the Woman's College, lay Buchanan Boulevard, for its first seven blocks a street of large and dignified old two-story houses adorned variously with columns, porticos, and generous porches, and guarded by sweetgums, maples, and oaks. After the campus wall turned abruptly west on Markham Avenue, Buchanan continued four blocks further north until it crossed Club Boulevard and passed open land to become Guess Road; but with the elevating college influence removed, the houses on those remaining four blocks became smaller, cozier, and more restrained in design. Exactly halfway between Markham Avenue and Club Boulevard stood our house, on property that had previously held an old brick and frame dwelling where my mother and her parents had lived briefly when they first moved to Durham; sixteen years later, after my parents had married and decided to build on the lot, the older house was torn down. (The wood was thriftily saved to build a house on my grandparents' farm.) Unfortunately some long-resident roaches remained in the dirt next to what became our half-basement; and no matter how immaculately my mother kept house thereafter, she could never completely drive out the bugs that held earlier title. Periodically, therefore, an exploring roach would find his way into the house, heralded by my anguished screams. Frozen with fear as I was, I could never summon up nerve enough to swat the intruder, so if my mother weren't around to kill him the roach ran free, if unnerved by the uproar.

My parents had built our house midway during the Depression, borrowing $4500 from the bank to pay for the construction, and reducing costs by using lumber cut from my grandparents' farm for the framing, rafters, and sills. A local carpenter directed the building; but each afternoon around three, after my father had finished his workday for Durham Public Service, he and my grandfather went over to labor until dark on the new house. When the building was completed in September my parents and grandparents moved in together, enjoying for the first time the luxury of living in a dwelling that boasted indoor plumbing, a coal furnace and radiators instead of fireplaces, a closet in each bedroom, and a new electric stove and refrigerator to replace the old wood stove and icebox. (Soon, too, a wringer washer would appear in the basement, eliminating the need for boiling clothes in iron pots over a fire.)

Only a block away, in a large, two-story, white frame house on Second Street, lived my widowed Great-Aunt Pat; and my grandmother Kittie, then seventy, rejoiced at being able once again to live close to her sister. Their reunion was sadly short: in mid-November, during the night that followed an unseasonably early snow, Kittie suffered heart failure and died in her sleep. My grandfather, still young and vigorous at fifty-five, continued to live with my parents for the two years that followed, occasionally walking the thirty-six miles to and from his Orange County farm. Finally he suggested delicately to his daughter that it was about time she and her husband started a family. A year later, shortly before my expected date of arrival, he married a tall, slender, attractive widow, his second cousin Allie Hall Stagg; the two stayed with my parents until my birth and then moved out to the farm, where they would live for the next twenty-two years.

Our house was a Tudor-styled brick cottage, solidly built according to my father's and grandfather's exacting specifications, and large enough by middle-class standards of the day that visitors stopped by throughout its construction. The rooms were small, but we had three bedrooms and a bath, living and dining rooms, a sun parlor, a kitchen with separate pantry and breakfast room, a covered side porch, a small screened back porch, and an attic and basement. A brick garage that held our 1934 Plymouth with room to spare stood behind the back yard; between the garage and our garden ran The Alley, a quiet path on which one could walk safely and usually unnoticed all the way through the block to B Street, stealing casual glances into the neighbors' back yards on the way. I liked our address: "Buchanan Boulevard" sounded dignified and grand, and in fact the house itself always seemed impressive to me, not so much on account of its size as because its elevation was well above street level so that you had to climb two flights of brick steps, separated by a short walkway, to reach the front door.

I loved the house with its substantial-looking brick exterior, its handsome wood floors, cheerful sun parlor, and pretty blue-tiled bathroom (that could never be locked, because we'd once had a nervous young roomer who had shut herself securely in and then fainted; alarmed by the incident, my mother had within the week persuaded my father to remove the lock). Only one flaw marred my paradise: I lived in terror of the living room chandelier. That wasn't because I feared the fixture might fall but because I was certain it was evil, the dwelling place of some nameless but powerful menace that threatened only me. Furthermore, it managed magically to conceal its wicked nature under an entirely ordinary, innocent-looking appearance. It was in fact disarmingly attractive in typical 1930's style: moderate-sized, with a bronze center that was surrounded by five opaque, pale green, flower-bordered glass shades. How I'd first become aware that the fixture was evil, I have no idea. Perhaps a long-forgotten dream had warned me, or maybe my knowledge had arisen spontaneously out of some longstanding, amorphous unease. But evil it was.

That was how it happened that for several years I avoided going through the living room alone (somehow I'd divined that the chandelier held no danger for me if someone else were present). Thus, if I needed to go from the dining room to the mailbox at the front (a journey of no more than twenty feet for the ordinary, unimperiled person), I went back through the kitchen and out the kitchen door to walk all the way across the back yard, down the length of the house, across the front yard, and finally up the flight of steps leading to the front door. This route was awkward and inefficient at best, especially when it was raining, and inevitably occasions arose when I was absolutely obliged to cross the living room. At such times I took a deep breath, averted my eyes, and dashed through the room at full speed. This aberrant behavior continued for several years, to the considerable wonderment and concern of my parents, who nevertheless spared my feelings by remaining tactfully silent. Eventually time solved the problem: the light fixture's power gradually declined, while simultaneously my panic faded; and finally by the time I was twelve I was able to saunter carelessly through the living room, casting an insouciant (though still watchful) glance at the chandelier as I crossed the room at a recklessly slow pace.

Besides the menacing fixture, the living room held our radio, which towered a foot or so above me when I sat in front of it listening to Jack Benny and Phil Harris on Sunday evenings. Over the mantel hung a framed calendar reproduction of Maxfield Parrish's enigmatic "Daybreak"; in front of the fireplace stood a card table picturing a splendid clipper ship under full sail. (Because of the tiresomely constant wood-fetching that had marked my parents' farm childhoods, only the coldest nights brought our fireplace into use.) Our built-in bookcase held a thick green leatherette volume authoritatively titled *The Modern Home Physician,* together with a biography of Will Rogers, a red clothbound *Hiawatha,* Charles Lindbergh's *We,* and cellophane-bonded Pocket Book editions of *Chicken Every Sunday,* Ernie Pyle's *Here Is Your War,* and (somewhat inexplicably, and probably left by a roomer) Gabriel Chevallier's racy *Scandals of Clochemerle.* (Our family Bible stayed not in the bookcase but on a nearby table, for easy access.) From a door-to-door salesman we had acquired a bright blue volume entitled *Children,* a tedious religious publication that I tried for years, but without success, to read; and we also had a paper-bound *Dr. Pierce's Dream Book,* from which I learned that dreaming of bees prefigured success in business, and that Dr. Pierce's Pleasant Pellets provided a peerless remedy for gas. My parents had thought their bookcase unusually generous in size when they built the house, but then they hadn't expected to produce a child who accumulated books with such reckless abandon; through the years our shelves slowly filled and overflowed with chronicles of the Bobbsey Twins and Nancy Drew, who later on found themselves uneasily sharing their space with E. E. Cummings, Samuel Beckett, and *The Palm-Wine Drinkard.* By the time I finished college, books had proliferated onto every flat surface in the living room, from whence they'd proceeded to stake out several locations in my bedroom. At last it became clear that our only hope of regaining a grip on this unruly wordhoard lay in a move to larger quarters; as matters stood, prospects for order looked dimmer by the day.

Beside the bookcase was the easy chair where my father sat each evening after dinner to read the *Herald.* Sometimes after he'd finished his newspaper I begged for shadow pictures, whereupon he would obligingly produce on the wall a dog, a donkey, a rabbit wiggling its ears. Other times he grasped me by my ankles and lifted me high into the air while I confidently held my knees stiff and straight, and reached for the ceiling. Finally, though, an evening came when as he started to lift me, my legs crumpled and I clutched anxiously at his shoulders for safety; understanding, he held me close for a moment before telling me sadly, "I can't lift you any more." Years later I arrived home from school one afternoon to find him not working in the yard as was his custom, but sitting motionless in his easy chair, feverish and ill with a kidney infection. A blanket covered him from shoulder to toe; but mine was the deeper chill.

We had our family meals in the breakfast room, where a brightly colored oilcloth covered the table that stood across from our Frigidaire. With their southern exposure the windows in that room were perfect for growing plants, and a row of African violets usually lined the sills. The dining room was for dressed-up company entertaining of the sort that required an embroidered white tablecloth and matching napkins together with our flowered china, heavy silver, and Indian Tree crystal. Also in the dining room stood our black upright piano, a gift from my grandfather to my mother in exchange for her solemn promise to eschew snuff; on the piano's music rack rested a Cokesbury Hymnal and my John Thompson lesson books, along with "Don't Fence Me In" and "The Lamplighter's Serenade," and "Drowsy Moon" from a piano recital. Hanging above the buffet were the two colorful still lifes of fruit that my grandmother had received years before as dividends with purchases of Cloverine Salve: because she and my grandfather owned no pictures other than a few family photographs, the prints had been her pride. Ennobled by the ornate frames she had somehow managed to acquire for them, they had accompanied her during the move from the farm into town, and then — eighteen years later — into this, her last home.

# THE WALLS WERE STRONG

On the spattered linoleum floor of our kitchen stood a large, cushioned oak rocker where my mother sat to cap strawberries, peel peaches, and shell beans; the chair stayed in front of a cabinet that contained not one but two conveniently built-in ironing boards, one of standard size for shirts and dresses, and a smaller one for sleeves. Despite my fondness for this built-in luxury that I considered one of the glories of our house, I usually stayed warily away from the board itself, because once when my mother had momentarily turned away from ironing I jerked inquisitively at the cord and pulled the hot iron down onto my foot, causing a painful burn that took weeks to heal. Along with this distasteful memory, the prospect of fire always frightened me; and my fears reached a fever pitch when Mary came in to help with an accumulation of ironing. Mary had an alarming habit of occasionally resting her hot iron on the cloth-padded board rather than on the metal holder, and each time she did, I envisioned hideous ruin and combustion. The cloth pad began to smolder — then ignited — then set our house instantly ablaze: flames twenty feet high engulfed the brick walls, crackling dreadfully, and parching my skin, taking my breath with their heat. Tormented by my horrible imaginings, I fretted long and anxiously over whether I should maintain an uneasy vigil over events in the kitchen, or leave the room gracefully and try to forget the whole thing. Since I was incapable of doing the latter, I finally mustered up nerve enough to mention the peril of her practice to Mary, who for some thirty years had ironed skillfully, uneventfully, and without benefit of my advice. On hearing my stammered, awkward hint she regarded me amiably, meanwhile resting her hot iron on the board, and advised, "Child, don't trouble yourself about things that ain't gonna happen." After that I worried in silence.

Next to the stove stood my grandmother's straight oak chair where, one summer afternoon while my mother napped, I decided to cut my hair. Thereupon I sat down, grasped the scissors firmly, and cut methodically for several minutes — one side only, but in some spots practically to the scalp. When my mother rose from her nap to view the result, she wept for the rest of the day. That evening I suffered the indignity of having the rest of my hair shorn in a futile attempt to match the part I'd cut; and ever after, whenever I complained that one side of my hair wouldn't behave properly, I received a gentle reminder about the time I'd cropped it so mercilessly. On the other side of the stove hung a string of dried red peppers; next to the peppers an omniscient Fidelity Bank calendar predicted the weather for each day of the year, indicated the moon's phases for planting, and showed the signs of the zodiac. When I became older I erred in having a wisdom tooth extracted without first consulting the bank's oracle to discover the "sign," which turned out to be in the head. For my negligence I developed a dry socket, missed three semester exams, and suffered miserably for a week.

The breakfast room opened onto a hall that contained a wall niche built especially to house our telephone, a functional black, four-party-line model that my mother and father answered with a pleasant, inquiring "All right?" The hall was too narrow to place a chair next to the phone, but that didn't matter because no one was expected to use the instrument long enough to sit down anyway. This unspoken rule was first breached when, at the age of three, I learned to dial my Uncle Sam's number: charmed by my new skill, I thereafter called him every morning before he left for work. Unfailingly kind and patient with children, Uncle Sam was always surprised and delighted to hear my voice; for my part, I felt pleased and happy at being able to enrich his life with my calls. I never noticed that after I had unnecessarily identified myself and we'd both assured ourselves of each other's good health, conversations tended to trail off into brief observations punctuated by long, companionable silences. Fortunately Uncle Sam never noticed either.

THE WALLS WERE STRONG

Down the hall from the telephone was the linen closet with
its shelves of white sheets and blue towels, its hamper of clothes
awaiting Monday — when they could be washed — and the
rag barrel, where I could rummage methodically and happily
through a rainbow of clothes history. Wornout linens,
threadbare and outgrown garments all found their way sooner
or later to the barrel, together with fabric remnants from the
dresses, blouses, and skirts my mother had sewn for herself
as well as for me and my dolls. Here were scraps of green and
blue gabardine from my school jumpers; remnants of crisp
yellow organdy from my first long dress, carefully stitched for
me to wear for my "Fluttering Butterflies" piano recital duet
with Eleanor Cowan; pale blue net and matching poplin, left
over from the ballet costume I'd worn to turn cartwheels with
Grace Hess into a school performance in Watts Street School's
gym; my wornout pink-flowered cotton flannel pajamas;
maroon poplin and green plaid chambray remnants from school
dresses; scraps of a yellow-flowered blue cotton flour sack that
had been transformed into a sunsuit; a length of clinging,
discreetly-patterned blue rayon from a Sunday dress of my
mother's; green Dan River cotton from my favorite sundress
(underpants to match, so that I could boldly turn handsprings
on the school playground without first checking to make sure
no boys were sneaking looks). A few scraps of white batiste
from my baby doll's long dress were there as well, and
sometimes I could find treasures — snippets of lace, a few inches
of narrow satin ribbon, a scrap of velvet — to hoard in my
miniature cedar chest, or else to create elaborate birthday or
Valentine's cards for my mother. And when I could get past
the fascination of the rag barrel to climb the wall stairway at
the back of the closet, the attic offered boxes of old dresses,
shoes, and hats that were splendid for dressing up; after I'd
rummaged through and properly attired myself, I came back
downstairs, set my small table with my pastel tea set, and

entertained my dolls with milk, cookies, and my best company manners.

The basement was my father's domain. There he kept his shotguns, boots, and hunting clothes, neatly organized and always put away clean in their own wooden cabinet; there too he kept his "yard clothes," and each afternoon on arriving home from work he descended the stairs with his slow, careful tread to change from his uniform before going out to mow the lawn, weed the flower beds, or work in his vegetable garden. At dusk he came back into the basement, this time to shower and put on clean clothes for dinner, which at our house was supper. With its shower, toilet, and large laundry sinks (a tin dipper hung on the wall for anyone who wanted a drink), the basement served to lighten the demands on our one tiny bathroom: as well as using the facility himself, my father occasionally allowed favored male roomers to shower downstairs instead of taking tub baths in the bathroom. (Female roomers were never accorded this privilege.)

Also in the basement was our wringer washer, where my mother spent most of each Monday washing clothes before carrying them in baskets to the back yard, where they were stretched taut with wooden pins on the clothesline to dry in the sun. (On rainy Mondays clothes dried on a line in the basement: irrespective of weather, the Wash on Monday schedule remained firm.) Normally I preferred to stay out of the basement because parts of it, particularly the staircase, were dark and frightening; but as long as my mother was working there it was safe for me to descend the stairs and join her. Once securely there, I could remain even after her departure and spend hours poring over old *Ladies' Home Journals*, *Woman's Home Companions*, and *McCall's*, reading their stories about career girls who discovered that all they really wanted was to get married and keep house, about young wives who were being driven to distraction by their children (but only briefly,until they met a smartly-dressed career woman who confessed that she'd give anything to be in their place, with a husband, a house, and babies), about marriages that were strengthened when husbands' old girl friends (usually career women) moved back to town. Best of all were the stories of enchantment, the ones about plump, grey-haired little fairy godmothers who transformed everyday objects into fresh, charming prom dresses, and about young boys who impetuously changed stern teachers into rabbits and then suffered agonies of responsibility and guilt. Sorcery had its uses, it seemed; but it was advisable to keep the upper hand.

From the stories I turned to Articles, Features, and Columns. I always checked to see whether Eleanor Roosevelt was talking about teenage pregnancy or anything else of interest in "If You Ask Me," whose crisp, starched tone implied delicately but unmistakably that despite her good will in offering solutions to readers' personal problems, the former First Lady's primary interests lay in weightier concerns, such as the U.N. I studied the Pond's ads, with their Astor, Vanderbilt, and Gould beauties who were invariably gifted harpists or violinists, accomplished linguists, sparkling hostesses, former officers in the WAVES, and daughters of "one of our greatest families." If the magazines weren't too old, I looked for coupons that I could mail off for Trushay lotion samples, or sterling silver Neptune's Daughter pins, or a trial bottle of Drene shampoo. I skipped the dull articles, the ones about "Your Colicky Baby" and "Meriden, Connecticut's Answer on Housing," in favor of the Sub-Deb column and features about Ingrid Bergman; and once in a while I came across something that seemed vital enough to cut out and save for future reference. Into this latter category fell such revelations as an article about college men's preferences in women, which disclosed that the men preferred girls with shoulder-length hair, 34-24-34½ measurements, and faces radiating sweetness and warmth. My hair, though technically shoulder-length, was on the dull and stringy side, and thirty-four inch bust and hip measurements seemed a star beyond my grasp; but I did practice radiating sweetness and warmth in the direction of my dresser mirror for the next two weeks.

*Better Homes and Gardens* and *The American Home* were less fun than *McCall's* and the *Companion,* being short on college men and fairy godmothers, and long on slipcovers, home heating systems, and lawn chairs; still, I could usually manage to find a few pictures of glamorous rooms for my Dream House Scrapbook, and most of the home magazines offered the stunning full-page color Armstrong's ads with their breathless accounts of young wives who, though struggling bravely on a pittance after their husbands' return from the war, contrived cannily with the aid of Armstrong's Linoleum to acquire the kitchen or powder room of their dreams. When I finally tired of reading magazines, I could rummage through our old trunk and gaze at my grandmother's long grey wool wedding dress, white kid gloves, and initialed silk handkerchief. And once for a few weeks my mother kept a hundred fluffy, pale yellow baby chicks in a pen close to the furnace, where they could stay safely warm: whenever I went down to see them they peeped contentedly, pecked daintily at their feed, and took one drop of water at a time in their beaks, turning up their heads to let the liquid run down their throats. For them I braved the dark stairs several times a day.

\* \* \* \* \*

Our yard was a rainbow of flowers, most of them fragrant: pink peonies that my grandmother and her sister had dug up and moved from the yard of the old house; white lilies-of-the-valley, red and yellow roses, pink sweetheart roses, white bridal wreath, blue and pink hyacinths, bright yellow forsythia, lavender lilacs, golden daffodils, purple and white iris, white gardenias, coral japonica, purple violets, and the tiny, brown, sweet shrubs that we liked to pick and let wilt until they smelled like ripe strawberries. Two huge crepe myrtles, one pink and one fuchsia, bloomed splendidly each June next to the street in front of our house; purple wisteria vines wound in and out of our back fence; ivy flourished along the brick that banked the lower flight of steps to our front door. Together with our profusion of flowers and shrubs my father grew apple, peach, and fig trees as well as pecans, scuppernongs, and Concord grapes. We even had an apricot tree that he had nursed carefully into bearing maturity despite the fact that apricots were seldom hardy enough to survive North Carolina winters. And every year on the vacant lot behind our house he planted a large garden that yielded basketsfull of juicy red tomatoes, butterbeans, okra, yellow squash, pole beans, potatoes, cantaloupes, cabbage, and white corn. My mother canned and preserved, and later froze, so many vegetables and fruits that she scarcely ever had to depend on Piggly Wiggly for produce; and between spring and fall the times were few when she was unable to pick flowers or fruit from our yard to take to a neighbor, or to use for ourselves.

Though I was an only child, playmates were plentiful. Back of our house, on Second Street, lived Jack Lester, whose front yard held a large, spacious umbrella tree, easy to climb and possessed of a fork of branches that formed a seat perfect for the two of us to sit in and eat chocolate marshmallow cookies, read comic books, and drink lemonade. In the block north of ours on Buchanan were the Morgan boys, the younger of whom occasionally entertained us girls by casually turning his back to direct an impressively high liquid arc into the shrubbery; across from the Morgans lived tall, slender Caroline Garrett, who reveled with me in the delicious excitement of a two-member secret society whose sole activity consisted of sending coded messages in tiny glass bottles, carefully deposited several times a day under the big mimosa tree on the corner. Down the street in the other direction I could play with Jean Poe, Ruth Jernigan, and sometimes Dickie Carter, who actually lived an hour away in Henderson but came over often to visit his grandmother, always bringing with him a satisfyingly large stack of comic books to trade. Next door to Dickie's grandmother, in a rambling white frame house with a wraparound porch, lived blond, handsome Billy Warren: we rarely met because he was several years my senior, but whenever we did he smiled and greeted me kindly, and I secretly idolized him long before he high-stepped and twirled his way into fame as a drum major — first for Durham High's marching band, afterwards as the state champion.

Across the street and beyond the Jernigans' house stood a white duplex, where Linda Hawley lived in one side and Janice Sue Rogers in the other: everyone liked them, though Janice Sue had an annoying habit of running home in tears to her mother whenever anyone hurt her feelings, which was about twice an hour. Between their duplex and the ones in which lived Angeline Norris and the Donahue girls, was an empty lot with a swing set that had end bars for climbing and playing Skin the Cat; and after I was old enough to leave my yard, it was there we most often gathered during the daytime. We were nearly always in motion — playing hopscotch on the sidewalk, turning cartwheels and handsprings, taking our turns jumping rope and turning for someone else, nonchalantly riding our bicycles without touching the handlebars, and racing, turning, coasting on our roller skates. Skating required some forethought, because you had to leave off your everyday Keds and wear substantial shoes with soles, preferably saddle oxfords, that could hold the metal toe clamps. And then you had to keep your skate key available to tighten or loosen the clamps every time you wanted to put on or take off your skates. Since hardly anyone's skate key ever fit anyone else's skates, losing your key was one of the most annoying things that could happen; and most of us wore ours on firmly knotted strings around our necks. Usually we just skated back and forth on our block, trying hard to dazzle each other by going directly from racing speed into a 180-degree turn; but when I became brave enough I coasted all the way down the steep, block-long hill north of our house, offhandedly luxuriating in the awed stares of those less brave.

Even in the daytime, when all our fathers were away at work, the neighborhood was a busy place. Most of our mothers came outside whenever produce salesmen drove down the street with their truckloads of watermelons and peaches, butterbeans and squash; and door-to-door salesmen frequently stopped by to offer encyclopedias, vacuum cleaners, and Bibles. The Fuller Brush man made his rounds every few weeks, and no matter how busy she was my mother always took the time to sit politely and study his catalogue, after which she bought a dollar vegetable brush or whisk broom, so the salesman wouldn't have wasted his time. The postman delivered mail twice each day (three times — Sundays included — during the Christmas holidays, when cards arrived from everyone we knew): the afternoon mail, though, contained mostly circulars, while morning brought the mail of note, letters and greeting cards that the senders had considered important enough to seal and put a three-cent stamp on rather than leave unsealed for only a penny. Twice a week the Durham Dairy man came by early in the morning to pick up empty bottles and leave fresh milk in the metal box on our front stoop. And nearly every summer afternoon a tinkly music-box tune announced the arrival of the ice cream man, and then we all had to race for home to ask our mothers for nickels to buy fudgsicles, or banana popsicles, or Dixie cups of chocolate ice cream.

When I was small, our back yard held a sandbox for me to

play in with my tin bucket and shovel; after I was five or six years old the sandbox disappeared, but the yard still yielded wonders. The apple and peach trees burst into pink and white clouds each spring, and the pecan tree had one low limb that was perfect for Skin the Cat. Buddy and Spunky, my terriers, lived in the back yard, spending cold nights sheltered by the small house that concealed the chute to our cellar coal bin; and usually we owned two or three much-petted yellow or calico cats, more often than not accompanied by multihued kittens of uncertain lineage. The yard included an abundant crop of clover, and the hours I spent looking it over rewarded me not only with four-leaf specimens but five and six-leaf ones as well, all of which I diligently pressed between the pages of my Bible. My wooden swing hung from solid round posts that my father had erected just in front of the peach trees; and whenever I wanted a bird's eye view of the immediate environs I could climb the ladder that went up to the flat black tin roof on our garage. Usually I came back down nearly as black as the roof, but fortunately the color washed off.

In the flat, grassy, dandelion-dotted expanse of our front lawn, my friends and I spent endless summer days flinging each other into Statues, tantalizing with Simon Says, and taking gallops, grasshopper leaps, and Giant Steps. When showers came we donned bathing suits and played in the rain; when the weather was hot and dry, we hopped and skipped under the hose. We jumped down the front brick steps, leapt across the walkway, and minced elegantly along the brick wall at the foot of the yard. Occasionally we tried, with singularly slight success, to walk on Caroline's stilts, which my mother persisted in calling Tomwalkers. When we needed a few minutes' rest we picked dandelion puffballs and blew away the seeds, or made clover chains, or stripped the middle petal off violets to reveal the tiny man seated inside, or lay flat on our backs (thus acquiring a persistent and maddening grass-itch) and scrutinized the sky for cloud pictures. Usually I saw kittens, angels, fairies, and dwarves; Dickie saw dogs, horses, and trucks; Caroline saw flowers and trees. Jean Poe once insisted she saw Jesus talking with the elders in the temple, but no one believed her.

If I wanted to go outside my own yard for entertainment I could walk a few steps down the back alley to where Mr. Barnes, our next-door neighbor, kept his goats. Usually he had two or three grown females, all bearing Biblical names — Mary, Martha, Rachel — as well as a billy; all of them coexisted happily, and the females begat baby goats with pleasing regularity. They were clean and healthy animals, the privileged possessors of a large fenced enclosure to ramble in during the day, and a cozy white frame house to sleep in at night. Mr. Barnes even donned a spotless white cotton jump suit with matching beret to feed and care for them; and if anyone living nearby were ever ungracious enough to complain about his unorthodox, four-footed neighbors, I never knew it. In addition to my good fortune in having goats for playmates, sometimes we drank fresh goat's milk, a rich and naturally homogenized liquid so bluish-white that Durham Dairy milk looked yellow by comparison. Mr. Barnes proudly supplied several satisfied customers with milk, and always he delighted in showing his animals to anyone who came to visit. Only rarely did the goats give him difficulties: once in a while he had to sit up all night with an ailing mother or baby, and one spring he was vexed by rodents that plundered the large bags of feed in his garage. Fortunately, though, our enterprising tortoiseshell cat quickly smelled out this promising new hunting ground; and once or twice a week thereafter we were summoned loudly and insistently to our back doorstep where, when we arrived, Skit Skat joyfully exhibited a large, dead rat. With this problem solved, Mr. Barnes's unusual hobby presented no further annoyances; and years later when he and his wife had decided to build a new house outside town, his first concern was to design for the chosen site a suitable pen for the goats.

Our house stood on the southwest corner of an intersection; since the other three lots on that corner were vacant except for trees and wild flowers, I had plenty of safe wilderness to explore. To the north lay two open fields that teemed with dandelions, bluebottles, goldenrod, and Queen Anne's Lace. Hundreds of tiny yellow and white butterflies swarmed there, darting and swooping joyously rather than drifting and hovering with the dignified grace of the large swallowtails in our yard. Few trees grew on those lots, except for one huge pecan tree and the lovely mimosa that not only served as Caroline's and my secret message depository, but also blossomed splendidly into fluffy red powder puffs each June. Directly facing our house, though, was a heavily wooded area that sloped sharply down to a tree-shaded creek; in the middle of that lot stood a thicket of plum trees with several low branches that made perfect horses for riding, or seats for daydreaming. Usually we played in the wooded part for a while, and then made our way to the bottom of the hill to pick pussy willows beside the creek. A culvert five feet or so tall carried water under the neighboring street, and if the creek were low we waded through the metal passage to the other side. Once we'd arrived and played around the tall, graceful weeping willow for a while, though, there was nothing much else to do except wade back through the drain to where we'd started. Our mothers' annoyance on discovering that we'd been playing in the culvert merely lent an additional fillip to the expedition, though it did us no good when we returned home with painful stone bruises from walking barefoot on the pebbles in the creek.

Since I wasn't allowed to leave our yard after dinner, during the long summer evenings all the other children on the block came to our house to play. After darkening the front of our house so as not to attract mosquitoes, my parents went out on the porch to rock contentedly, talk over the day's events, entertain neighbors who walked over, and watch us play Ain't-No-Bugar-Bears-Out-Tonight, which frightened me nearly to death. The adults kept an eye out for falling stars while we caught lightning bugs to go into a Mason jar with holes punched in the lid, where the insects lit up methodically for the rest of the evening; when everyone had to go home, we opened the jars and shooed the bugs out, thus assuring our supply for the next night. We had June bugs, too, which didn't sting but buzzed aggressively and resembled bumblebees too much for most of us to feel really comfortable with them. But one evening when I lay dejected and ill with an earache, too sick to go out and play, Sterling Brockwell kindly caught a June bug, tied him onto the end of a long string, and brought him into my bedroom to cheer me. Since Sterling's interests were already running toward airplanes and football, we had little to talk about, and I was all the more overwhelmed by his solicitude in coming to visit; together we watched the bug fly about, buzzing in noisy protest, for half an hour. When darkness approached, Sterling carefully pulled up the string until the shiny insect rested gently on one palm; then, sheltering it with his other hand, he went outside to release it into the warm, starlit night.

Though we could play outdoors nearly all year long, weather was frequently capricious, occasionally sharp. Forecasting was often inexact, so that summer brought violent and wholly unexpected thunderstorms that sent my mother and me scurrying around the house to close windows; winter offered rare snowstorms that were often more accurately predicted by the appearance of tiny snowbirds than by the weathermen. One Sunday morning in January, while my parents still slept, I walked sleepily to our front door to pick up the *Herald;* but when I pushed the screen door, it refused to open. Puzzled, I looked up and outside to discover that the yards, trees, and streets as far as I could see had been magically blanketed with white. The door was banked tightly shut by a six-inch snowfall that had come, quietly and without any warning at all, during the night.

Even two inches of snow, let alone six, constituted a major event in Durham. Because snow was a rarity rather than a way of life, the city owned no equipment with which to clear it away; any snow at all, therefore, usually resulted in the schools' closing for several days, delighting us children and irking our mothers. If, as usually happened, the temperature rose for a few hours and then dropped again so that the snow on the streets melted somewhat and then refroze, anyone unlucky enough to be driving fought a perpetual, though variable, battle against slush, ice, and slush again.

None of this troubled my friends and me, of course. We viewed snow as one of Nature's blessings, a miracle to be enjoyed to the fullest. As soon as I'd gulped down my Rice-Krispies and Ovaltine, swallowed my cod-liver oil, and struggled into my snowsuit and galoshes, I was outside for the day except for when hunger struck, or when I had to go to the bathroom. In our front yard Caroline and I lay on our backs in the snow and waved our arms up and down to make snow angels; jumping up, we threw snowballs at trees and at each other until we were tired. Then buckling down to serious work, we built a snowman, giving him small pieces of coal for eyes, a carrot for a nose, a dried red pepper for his mouth. We begged a scarf, hat, and broom from my mother for the finishing touches, stood back and admired our creation, and then headed for the steep hill just north of my house to go sledding. Neither of us owned a sled, but heavy pieces of cardboard served quite well to slide down on; if one of the Hurst boys brought their sled and joined us, so much the better.

When five o'clock and dusk arrived, we returned home cold, wet, exhausted, and happy beyond belief. After stripping off my soggy snowsuit, my mother deposited me into a hot tub filled with bubble bath, where I soaked for half an hour before languorously getting out to put on my pink flannel pajamas that had been warmed on the radiator. And after dinner, when my mother had mixed together milk, sugar, and vanilla, and my father had brought in a large platterful of fresh, clean snow to add to it, we ate snow cream that was scarcely more substantial than a moonbeam, but fluffy and delicious while it lasted. Enveloped in a cloud of warm, tired contentment, I felt my eyelids growing heavy, and began to think about going to bed. Tomorrow, my father promised, the snow would still be there.

*The Mountain Nymph, sweet Liberty;*
*And if I give thee honour due,*
*Mirth, admit me of thy crue*
*To live with her, and live with thee,*
*In unreproved pleasures free....*

— *John Milton*

# CHAPTER 3
# Pleasures Free

As did a number of other American cities during the early part of this century, for years Durham boasted a gay and glittering amusement facility: Lakewood Park, developed by Richard H. Wright of the Durham Traction Company, had opened to city-wide anticipation to become an immediate popular success. Initiating use of the park was the Mantoka Tribe #21, Improved Order of Red Men: on 4 July 1902 the *Morning Herald* reported on the group's barbecue of the preceding evening at "Lakeside Park," commenting that the dinner had been attended by some three hundred persons, most of whom rode the streetcars to the park and back home. Noted the *Herald,* "It was the first time that the park had been used." The *Durham Daily Sun* of that date also reported the barbecue, likewise calling the park "Lakeside"; three days later a tacit, graceful correction appeared:

> "Lakewood" is the name of the new park of the Traction Company, which will be opened to the public very soon. It is a pretty name — suggestive of a lake and woods — and both will be there.

A gala opening took place two weeks later, and although the park wasn't yet the many-faceted attraction it would later become, Durhamites were delighted. By June of the following year the merry-go-round and the bowling alley were in full operation, and on 14 June 1903 the *Morning Herald* announced that the newly-completed Casino would open the following evening with *Confusion!*, a "polite comedy" to be presented by the Wells Dramatic Company. Seven hundred or more persons attended the play, which the *Herald* afterward reported to have been "agreeably rendered." Following the play, the orchestra furnished music at the pavilion, where a number of enthusiastic couples danced until nearly midnight.

Built on some two dozen acres of beautifully landscaped property southwest of town, the park eventually offered in addition to the merry-go-round, casino, and dance pavilion, a roller coaster, roller skating rink, picnic ground with shelters, and a children's playground with swings, seesaws, and slides. Also in the park was Durham's first swimming pool, a mud-bottomed pond that was occasionally drained by mischievous boys who then captured frogs, turtles, and snakes in the mud. Later on, the original pond was replaced by a concrete pool; publicized extensively (City Water, Shower Baths, Instructor, Ladies' Maid, Water Changed Every Monday), the pool became immensely popular. Durham historian Wyatt Dixon relates the story of a prominent though absent-minded businessman, never seen without a derby hat on his head and a newspaper under his arm, who while strolling in the Park one warm afternoon was suddenly seized by the desire for a refreshing swim. As a women's Sunday-School class sedately picnicked close by, he went into the bathhouse to change his apparel; only a few minutes later, he walked back out to dive into the water. Screams filled the air: though the man was wearing his derby and carrying his newspaper as was his custom, he had neglected to don his bathing suit.

Events in the park were many and varied. For years the Runkel Stock Company presented nightly plays in the casino — *Dr. Jekyll and Mr. Hyde, Peg O' My Heart, Pollyanna,* and dozens of others. General Admission cost ten cents, Reserved Seats twenty cents; a child's admission cost ten cents anywhere in the house. (Ads for dramatic productions during those early years often sought to assuage patrons' lingering worries about the propriety of the theater by promising earnestly, "Our shows are entirely Free from anything that will offend you: High Class and Refined.") Such special events as Dare Devil Reichert in Sensational Balloon Ascensions drew excited crowds; watermelon slicings took place in the daytime, and fireworks displays at night. One summer's feature attraction was a diving horse that jumped twenty-five feet or so from a platform into a pool; adventurous souls could buy a ticket to ride down on the unlucky animal, and one couple who had just been joined in marriage on the platform rode the horse down together to celebrate.

Billed as "the Coney Island of the South" (thus prompting a man in another town to write requesting a room on the waterfront), Lakewood Park came alive with lights, music, and activity on weekends and holidays. Families picnicked; courting couples filled the dance pavilion; children crowded the swimming pool and merry-go-round; and everyone ate syrup-topped Razzle-Dazzle popcorn ("good for the ladies and good for the babies") at five cents a bag. Young people flocked into the zoo with its Texas Monster Reptiles, Tennessee Raccoon, and Belgium Hares from the Honolulu Islands; mothers had their children's pictures taken at the Electric Studio. On well-heralded special occasions the swimming pool's manager threw a few dollars' worth of silver coins into the pool, inviting everyone wearing bathing suits to dive for the money. During busy times the Durham Public Service Company put every one of its trolleys into use on the Lakewood route, and a new group of merrymakers, spilling out of the open-sided summer streetcars, arrived at the park every eight minutes. On quieter days business and civic groups used the park as a meeting place, and from time to time local churches conducted baptismal services in the old mud-bottomed swimming pool.

For over thirty years Lakewood prospered as Durham's only public recreational facility; but during the 1920's the Runkel Company discontinued its dramatic productions at the casino, and the park began a slow decline. By the early 1930's many people had acquired cars and were beginning to travel outside Durham on weekends. The park's equipment began to show signs of age, and attendance dwindled further still; though Lakewood's managers invested increasingly in advertising, and sponsored impressive special attractions, before World War II the once lively, exuberant park had closed. No trace of its gaiety remains — a 1960-vintage shopping center now stands sedately on the site — but for many Durhamites the words "Lakewood Park" still evoke a whirling, brightly-colored, musical memory.


Nothing ever came close to replacing the Coney Island of the South, though on occasion during the 1930's and 1940's the Recreation Department offered Durham children such modest diversions as birdhouse contests, kite-flying competitions, and "street showers." The latter were summertime events in which the Fire and Water Departments combined forces to offer watery respite from the heat: sprinklers were attached to fire hydrants in designated locations, and traffic in those areas was rerouted so that children could play in safety. North of Durham, Crystal Lake for a few years provided visitors with picnic areas and a place to swim, together with a miniature train on which a dozen or so children could ride around the lake.

Something more was needed, though, and soon after the war the Recreation Department, aided by the Hornaday Foundation, established the small Children's Museum that would quickly gain widespread community support: during the forty years since its inception the Museum has counted nearly every prominent person in Durham among its supporters, if not as a member of its governing board. (During the late 1940's the Kiwanis Club provided financial support for a time, producing its "Tune Time" minstrel for the project's benefit, while Gail Farthing and Nello Teer rode in the Meadow Brook Saddle Club show, the profits from which went to the Museum.) After its first year in Northgate Park the Museum moved into an old house on the Hillandale Golf Course; in 1962 it moved again, to its present home on Murray Avenue. Ten years later the institution was rechristened, becoming the North Carolina Museum of Life and Science. Today the Museum includes a prehistory trail and petting zoo together with a miniature railroad, a large reptile collection, participatory exhibits illustrating basic scientific principles, and an important, NASA-assisted exhibit featuring artifacts from America's journeys in space.

But in 1948 it was Durham's fledgling Children's Museum; and since it was conveniently located only a couple of miles from our house, I went there often. In the company of Melissa Shuler and the Arena children, I collected wild flowers, leaves, and redbug bites on Shaddassee, the Trail of Many Paths; learned to distinguish a sweet gum tree from a white oak; and petted the Museum's rabbits and goats as well as a white rat, which bit me. We braided lanyards, modeled paperweights and ashtrays in clay, practiced identifying bird calls, and contemplated the turtle pond. In the Do Something Club we created dolls' cradles out of oatmeal boxes; decorated paper bag masks; produced elaborate snowflakes by cutting designs out of folded squares of white paper; and made spatter pictures of every variety of leaf known to the Piedmont, managing in the process to cover ourselves thoroughly with paint.

The *Durham Morning Herald* provided generous coverage of the Museum and its activities, and one day Charles Cooper, the newspaper's photographer, came out and took Gabe Manassee's and my picture as we thoughtfully studied a case of mounted birds. Always recovering from one injury or another, just then I was sporting large bandages on my legs to protect the gentian-violet-covered scrapes that I'd acquired from swinging too long and too enthusiastically on the thick wooden swings in Johnny Stinespring's back yard. When the picture appeared in the newspaper two days later, I was mortified to discover that the edge of one of my bandages showed beneath my dress, bearing an embarrassing resemblance to a drooping slip and greatly detracting, I felt, from my attitude of scholarly solemnity as I inspected the birds. My mother listened patiently to my anguished wails and assured me no one would notice. I didn't believe her for a minute, being firmly convinced that everyone in town noticed and only out of delicacy were refraining politely from mentioning it. A year later the Museum included the picture in its glossy, sepia-and-cream promotional brochure, thus neatly preserving my humiliation for posterity.

The Museum offered something for everyone: if you didn't want to join the Art Club or the Nature Club, you could still look at the butterfly and shell collections and go on the treasure hunts and field trips. Most of us thought it a wonderland of delights; and being banished from its environs for bad behavior, as were a couple of the boys, was the worst punishment we could imagine. For anyone who couldn't get over to Northgate, the *Durham Sun* ran on its front page a daily Nature Museum News Corner in which Director Mary Lela Grimes discussed everything from butterflies to elephants, horned lizards to mushrooms. WDUK offered "From the Children's Museum" each Saturday morning; and once Gray Murdock, Charlie Sanders, Bobby Hopper, and I accompanied Miss Grimes and a squirrel to WDNC for a special radio broadcast that turned into near-disaster as the anxious animal escaped to investigate every piece of equipment in the studio. Later on, the Museum would sponsor an annual Christmas party for one of its most popular residents, Polly the Parrot, to which Durham children enthusiastically brought gifts of cracked corn, bird seed, rabbit and dog food, and peanuts to help with the expense of feeding the animals. (When Polly died at the age of thirty-six, the Museum was draped in black.)

Inspired by my contacts with the world of nature and especially by the Museum's collections, I became a collector myself, of butterflies. My parents bought me a net that I soon became proficient in wielding as I swooped down on unwary prospects; after getting the butterfly securely in hand I dropped on a little ammonia, pinned it to a piece of cardboard, and used strips of paper to secure its wings until they stiffened and the strips could be removed. Since Durham wasn't known for its variety of butterflies, all I ever collected were yellow and black swallowtails, together with an occasional orange and black Monarch. (The small yellow and white butterflies that filled the field across the street remained safe from my plunderings only because they seemed too numerous to be interesting.) Though I did look them up in my *Book of Knowledge* to find out their names, my interest in the butterflies was entirely unscientific: my only reason for collecting them was to make something beautiful my own. A couple of years were to elapse before it would dawn on me that despite their beauty against white cotton, the graceful beings were even lovelier alive and free. But finally, late one hot summer afternoon, I found a stunning Luna moth, pale green and delicate, clinging gently to the underside of a bean vine leaf in our garden; for once lacking the heart to disturb anything so fragile and rare, I left it untouched. My butterfly collecting days had ended.

* * * * *

Aside from church, my parents' social life (which was mine as well, babysitters being an expensive luxury) centered around The Gang, six or eight couples and a few single women who gathered frequently to cook hamburgers, roast hot dogs, or make ice cream — sometimes to celebrate someone's birthday or anniversary, more often just for the fun of being together. For my eighth birthday we cooked a picnic supper at Duke Park, but usually we gathered in someone's back yard. The men occupied a mysterious realm of employers, factories, and schedules that I considered of small interest; several of the women held jobs as well, but they talked of things I could understand, and their gaiety and charm captivated me whenever we met. Plump, jolly Ruth Riddick worked in her brother's grocery; pretty, redhaired Kathleen Reaves, stylish in her crisp piqué dresses, worked at Liggett and Myers, as did Lois Nichols and Becky Batten, two slender brunettes who chatted happily and sociably with everyone. Sometimes my cousin Skip joined us, fascinating the group with her vivacity and playing the piano for us to sing "Accentuate the Positive" while I dolefully contrasted her effortless chords and runs with my own playing, much of which consisted of painful battles with the onerous exercises in my *Hanon*. Only three children besides myself came to the parties — statuesque, auburn-haired Ann Markham and her brother Jimmy, who usually spent the evening bickering more or less good-naturedly, and quiet, handsome Paul Reaves, to whom I grandly referred (in his absence) as My Cousin, though the actual kinship was at best distant. A few years my senior, they nonetheless tolerated me agreeably; and while The Gang talked and joked, we spent our time transacting business (three Little Lulus equalled one Captain Marvel).

Sometimes we gathered at the Reaveses' house, where I felt grownup and important because Kathleen had invited me to call her by her first name; there, too, Paul let me read his Hardy Boys mysteries, and I could sit by the phonograph and play Nat King Cole and Frankie Laine records, "Ghost Riders in the Sky," and "Mona Lisa," and "Ballerina." Best of all were the parties given by John and Sallie Markham, who cared for a large farm belonging to a prominent local family. On those evenings The Gang met at the Markhams' house to drive through acres of apple orchards up to the very top of a high hill, where beside an arbor of scuppernongs and Concord grapes stood a stone gazebo. After we'd cooked our hamburgers, roasted Campfire marshmallows, and eaten chocolate cake and homemade ice cream, we sang everyone's favorite songs, "Carolina in the Morning," and "Down in the Valley," and "Shine On, Harvest Moon," until darkness fell, and — because the hill had no lights — the sky filled quickly with stars. Paul patiently helped me find Orion and the Milky Way, and soon afterwards we all went home.

Once or twice a year the social occasions took on a purpose as three or four couples sensibly joined forces to cook brunswick stew. Enlightened North Carolinians consider brunswick stew the staff of life, the sweetest taste of heaven this world can offer; it's prepared in as many different ways as there are cooks who make it, but my mother's recipe called for chicken, beef, onions, potatoes, tomatoes, butterbeans, corn, peas, and rice — and patience.[1] Preparing the ingredients took half a day: the women cooked and cut up the meats, chopped potatoes and onions, assembled the home-canned vegetables. That evening the group met at ours or the Reaveses' house and the women began the cooking, first boiling potatoes and onions in the chicken broth and then slowly, carefully adding the other vegetables and the meats, one at a time so that the delicious-smelling mixture never stopped simmering, always stirring, stirring, steadily and rhythmically, to keep the stew from sticking to the deep, navy blue enamel pots. (Brunswick stew was temperamental: if you tried to hurry it, it wouldn't be good; and if you left off stirring

[1]Some recipes require pork, others squirrel; one large-quantity recipe begins its list of eighteen ingredients with "15 gallons chopped potatoes, 12 gallons onions, and 50 pounds stew beef."

for even a few seconds, it would stick.) During the final hour the men took over the stirring; gradually the stew thickened and cooked down an inch or so, and first one and then all of the women would pronounce it done. Everyone had a ritual taste, but only a little, because we all knew (and someone always pointed out anyway) it would taste better the next day when the flavors had blended. Each couple took home their three or four quarts of the final product, and the next evening each of them would dine royally on brunswick stew, chopped onions, cole slaw, hush puppies, and Little Acorn barbecue. And for the next few days, whenever they talked with friends the women would find occasion to mention they'd just made a stew. Standard fare at church dinners it might be, but producing brunswick stew at home was an Event.

(The Gang's gatherings included coffee, iced tea, Cokes, and a Nu-Grape for me, but no beer; and in fact no one I knew drank alcohol. Out in the country some of my aunts made sweet scuppernong wine that they offered on holidays, but most people used wine only for cooking. My knowledge of alcohol was limited: fancies of being merry with the fruitful Grape hadn't yet swum into my ken, so that the substance I knew only as Whiskey was linked inextricably in my mind with vice and turpitude. One dreadful day when I walked into our pantry to get out the cooky press, I was horror-struck to discover a bottle of cooking wine, about a third empty — probably from evaporation — and darkened with age. My heart sank. Could one of my parents be a secret drinker? Would our home be Destroyed by Whiskey? Worry haunted me for weeks, during which time I edgily sneaked into the pantry each day to examine the bottle for a telltale indication that one of my parents was covertly drinking from it, perhaps in the night when the rest of us were asleep. To my immense relief, though, the wine level stayed constant throughout the time I watched. Gradually the specter of Whiskey faded, at last vanishing entirely. When we moved from the house fourteen years later, my mother threw out the wine.)

At home, entertainment meant our radio. Monday nights we tuned in to *Lux Radio Theatre;* before that had come *Inner Sanctum,* whose creaking door frightened me so badly I could never muster the courage to listen. Tuesdays we joined Fibber McGee and Molly at 79 Wistful Vista, where the black maid answered her summons by bellowing, "Somebody bawl fo' Beulah?"; Myrt, the telephone operator, said nothing at all; and each week we waited eagerly for the moment when Fibber opened the door to his hall closet, enabling his accumulation of household paraphernalia to crash noisily to the floor. Wednesday evenings brought kindly, sympathetic Dr. Christian, who stayed so busy solving people's personal problems that some cynics wondered when he found the time to practice medicine; after Dr. Christian came *Duffy's Tavern,* "where the elite meet to eat, Archie da manager speakin', Duffy ain't here." (Archie was frequently visited by "the mucous of an idea," but Duffy never appeared.) Thursdays, Mr. Keen Traced Lost Persons; Fridays, Fanny Brice brought us mischievous Baby Snooks, forever and expertly adding fuel to the flames of her parents' fights. Saturdays offered Ralph Edwards M.C.ing *Truth or Consequences,* which once kept us and the rest of the country puzzled for weeks as to the identity of the Walking Man. (He turned out to be Jack Benny, walking because he was too miserly to ride a bus.)

Sundays, though, were best of all. Afternoon brought The Shadow, in reality wealthy man-about-town Lamont Cranston, who years before in the Orient had learned how to cloud men's minds so that they could not see him; assisted by his friend and constant companion the lovely Margot Lane, each week

Cranston used his mysterious power to aid the forces of law and order by thwarting evil scientists or power-mad leaders. At six in the evening North Carolinians tuned in virtually *en masse* to hear *Carolina Chats,* Carl Goerch's folksy stories about their state and the people in it; after *Chats,* the Sunday evening lineup began in earnest. Hapless Jack Benny was besieged by train announcers, unctuous floorwalkers, the Sportsmen Quartet, Ronald and Benita Coleman, Fred Allen, and a holdup man demanding his money or his life, thus throwing Benny into the longest pause of anguished indecision in the history of radio. Our Miss Brooks dealt capably with the vicissitudes of high school English students, all the while maintaining her tireless pursuit of Mr. Boynton, the bashful biology teacher; impudent Charlie McCarthy ogled pretty girls and needled Edgar Bergen about moving his lips when Charlie talked.

And there was Durham's own offspring, *Amos 'n' Andy.* The show had actually begun as *Sam 'n' Henry;* created by Freeman Gosden and Charles Correll a few years after their initial meeting at the Academy of Music, the program first aired on 12 January 1926. Two years later Gosden and Correll left WGN, the *Chicago Tribune* radio station where the show had begun, to join a station that was willing to develop the program nationally. But since the title itself remained the property of the *Tribune,* the authors created new characters and a new title; and on 19 March 1928 *Amos 'n' Andy* first appeared.

The title characters were two Harlem blacks who owned the Fresh Air Taxi Company, which derived its name from the fact that the company's sole, aged asset had no windshield. At the height of the show's popularity during the 1930's, virtually the entire country listened: theater marquees advertised that their films would be stopped each evening at 7 so that *Amos 'n' Andy* could be piped in; taxis and buses had no passengers; and utility records showed that few people ran water or flushed toilets while the program aired. (Auto theft, though, increased as thieves came to realize that in any household they chose, chances were the entire family was sitting around the radio.) Events on the series received extensive press coverage: when Amos went on trial for murder, the case was discussed and debated in newspapers throughout the land.

By the time I was old enough to listen, the show had become a half-hour weekly program, and steady, reliable family man Amos had receded into the background in favor of colorful, conniving George Stevens. Better known as The Kingfish of his lodge, the Mystic Knights of the Sea, Stevens spent most of his time trying to ensnare slow-witted Andy in some scheme whose ultimate goal was the relocation of Andy's cash into The Kingfish's pocket. Madame Queen, who several years before had nearly succeeded in marrying Andy during a program that made national headlines, still made occasional appearances; Sapphire Stevens and her mother railed weekly at the Kingfish; Lightnin' shuffled through life at a languid crawl, promising, "Yazzuh — I'll just whiz right on over deah." And each Christmastime Andy's small daughter Arbadella asked her father the meaning of the Lord's Prayer; and with gentleness and grace, Andy explained.

*Amos 'n' Andy* included no Uncle Toms: Gosden and Correll developed their characters with care and affection, and the show's humor dwelt in personality traits rather than in racial stereotypes. Still, like *The Green Pastures,* the program was a product of older attitudes and thought. Ultimately it couldn't survive the strengthening black movement; protests by the NAACP helped to remove it from the air. But at its peak it was probably the most popular radio show ever broadcast; and in 1933, when George Bernard Shaw was ending his tour of the United States to return to England, he reflected, "There are three things I'll never forget about America: the Rocky Mountains, Niagara Falls, and *Amos 'n' Andy.*"

\* \* \* \* \*

# HEAVEN FOR BEGINNERS

My mother didn't work. Having left her job at the hospital a year before my birth, she waited till I entered high school to go back; and even then she only filled in for others, staying a few weeks or months as she was needed. Instead of working she managed to keep busy with sweeping and waxing wood floors; dusting and polishing furniture; mopping and waxing kitchen linoleum; vacuuming rugs, washing windows, and scrubbing the bathroom; washing down porches and walls; washing, starching, and ironing clothes; cooking meals and washing dishes; baking cakes, pies, and cookies; canning and freezing vegetables and fruits; and making preserves, jellies, and jams. In addition she cooked and baked for our neighbors and friends when someone died or was ill; shopped for our household supplies and groceries; sewed dresses, playclothes, and school costumes for me, and mended for all of us; drove me to music lessons, the library, and the Children's Museum; taught Sunday-School and belonged to a church circle; handled the family finances; and drove to and from her father's farm — then a forty-five minutes' trip — at least twice a week, and occasionally every day. To add a bit of extra income to my father's salary she took in roomers; sometimes, too, she sold produce from my grandfather's farm: fresh brown eggs, country butter molded into neat round shapes that had strawberries imprinted on the top, and — in December, after hog-killing — homemade sausage, fragrant and rich with sage.

When she baked, I helped. Determinedly I creamed butter and sugar for cakes until the mixture became light and fluffy, and my arms ached; poured oil drop by drop to mix mayonnaise so good that none of us could bear the taste of the commercial kind; broke the tiny capsule of food coloring inside the plastic bag of Nucoa and then squished, squeezed, kneaded until the margarine obediently darkened from pasty white to a smooth, healthy yellow. It was my job, too, to pour the cream off each bottle of milk so my father and mother could have it for their

90

coffee. Chocolate chip cooky dough was mine to mix as I waited eagerly for the moment when I could pour in all the flour at once and then stir slowly, until bit by powdery bit the honey-colored dough reappeared. At Christmastime I grated coconut for cakes, or helped pull fondant until it became creamy and could be cut into mints, or else folded walnuts and candied pineapple into a small mountain of batter, for fruit cake. The aluminum cooky press was the most fun of all: you held it at just the right angle to the cooky sheet and moved it slowly along, first turning the knob at the top clockwise, and then quickly reversing it to push out the dough into perfectly ridged shapes that would bake golden, delicately edged with brown.

One or two afternoons a week, after my mother had finished her housework and cooking for the day, we went somewhere special. Sometimes we walked down Buchanan Boulevard — she on the sidewalk, I balancing on top of the stone wall surrounding Duke's East Campus — to the south end of the campus where two giant magnolias, their limbs two or three feet apart, invited climbing. Blithely confident of my sure-footedness, my mother sat on a nearby bench to read while I happily worked my way up through the branches, occasionally passing a bird's nest, until at twenty or twenty-five feet I paused to peer underneath me through the foliage, prudently decided I was high enough, and started back down. Before we left I checked The Sower, the larger-than-lifesize statue a few feet away, to see whether any coins lay in the outstretched hand that was just low enough for me to peer into; usually a couple of pennies rested there, but since I longed to believe they had materialized by magic, I left them alone.

(Along with its magnolias, Duke offered other entertainment. Each spring my parents took me to the Engineering Show, where we viewed an assortment of inventions that put the principles of engineering into more or less practical use: we liked the talking garbage cans, but decided television offered little promise. At the Women's Gym, the Nereidians presented graceful, precise water ballets; and once my mother took me to Branson Theatre to see *Othello* acted in the round. [Afterward, trying to find decorous answers to my inconvenient questions, she clearly regretted this excursion into Culture.] Within easy walking distance of our house stood the East Campus Dope Shop, which mixed some of the best milkshakes around. Once in a while we went over to West Campus to visit the oddly-named Duke Chapel, a cathedral-sized Gothic structure whose front doorway and the two windows

*Postcard view of Duke Chapel, ca. 1936.*

above formed a great, amazed face.[2] And each Easter Sunday afternoon, armed with our black Kodak, the three of us went in our Easter finery to visit Duke Gardens, walking all the way down the wooded path to the goldfish pond and then up the stone steps on the other side, through terraced rows of tulips and iris and pansies, past Japanese cherry and crabapple trees, bright yellow forsythia, and ethereal white spirea, then past two fountains to the purple-wisteria-clad gazebo at the very top of the hill. Outside the gazebo we all stood solemnly against the boxwoods so an obliging passerby could snap our picture; then back down the steps, with a last look at the tulips and the goldfish pond, to return home.)

Sometimes after leaving the magnolias in the afternoons we walked by the King's Daughters Home, where I watched breathlessly for a glimpse of a golden-haired princess wearing a long dress and a crown: it was a heavy disappointment to discover that the Home's residents were elderly ladies who, though charming and kind, dressed in street clothes much like my mother's and wore no crowns at all. If we wanted to go further, we walked on to the tranquil, grassy park that occupied a whole city block at the corner of Main and Duke Streets. There we could stroll through the paths that were shaded by oaks and maples, or else sit on the wooden benches to rest; from any spot in the park we could gaze up at the large cedar that during the evenings at Christmastime was so splendidly lit that people drove by in a steady stream to see. When I was twelve, though, we read in the *Herald* one morning that a new tobacco research laboratory would be built on that property, and soon afterward the park disappeared.

If we waited till my father had come home from work, we could use our Plymouth to go further afield. Occasionally we drove over to Erwin Auditorium, which had been built early

[2]Durham's City Directory for 1929 referred to the Chapel, then in its planning stage, as "a rural church near the city."

in the century as a recreational center for the textile workers living close by in small frame houses that they rented from the mill (twenty-five cents per room, per week); by now few of the Auditorium's recreational offerings remained except for the small, nearly deserted library, but there I could dream over L. M. Montgomery's *Emily* books, with their talented, beautiful heroine who was mysteriously gifted with second sight. Once or twice a month we went to Watts Hospital, where my mother happily greeted friends she'd worked with years before, and then disappeared into one of the big open wards to visit a friend or relative, usually discovering in the course of her visit that one or two other acquaintances were on the same ward, and she could visit them as well. Meanwhile I wandered up and down the hospital's sunny corridors, modestly averting my eyes from the patients who occupied temporary beds in the halls, and peering out the tall windows to look for goldfish in the courtyards' reflecting pools; when three o'clock arrived, I climbed the stairs to Ward A, Maternity, to gaze through the glass at the new babies. If it weren't too close to dinnertime when we left the hospital, we crossed the street to Aubrey's Drink Stand for a hot dog, or else went to the Hospital Pharmacy where we could sit in comfortable booths and have cherry Cokes or ice cream. A quick stop by the Rolling Pin for chocolate eclairs, and then back home, where my father met us as we drove in.

To replenish such routine daily staples as milk, bread, and popsicles, I could walk to the Welches' Watts Street Grocery only a block east of our house, or else to Mr. Gresham's store in back of us; but once a week we took our car to buy groceries at the Piggly Wiggly on Main Street, and then I got to spend a few minutes in Sawyer & Moore (Durham's Predominating Store), between the Piggly Wiggly and the Donut Dinette.

Nominally a drugstore, Sawyer's in fact offered everything from Iodent toothpaste, Blue Horse notebook paper, and Esterbrook pens to Cara Nome hand cream, Lilt home permanents, and Musterole. But the store's real drawing card was its soda fountain, and I loved watching the bobby-soxers who rushed in after school to crowd into booths — sip on ice cream sodas — giggle, squeal, and flirt. In between observing and eavesdropping I looked through *Seventeen, Calling All Girls,* and *Screen Stories* at the magazine rack. *True Confessions* and *True Romance* were there as well, but of course you didn't want to be seen buying one of those, and even less did you want to have one in your possession, especially at home; if you weren't obvious about it, though, you could do a good bit of reading while you stood at the magazine rack. The key was to remain standing: sitting down on the floor telegraphed the news that you were settling down to read for quite a while, and the salespeople didn't like that.

When I was in the ninth grade, a "Zesto" opened in a tiny building back of Sawyer's, creating a minor sensation as it offered Durham's first taste of soft ice cream. We watched, fascinated, as the creamy mixture curled out of a substantial, clinical-looking stainless steel dispenser, to be twirled round on a cone and then dipped into a liquid chocolate or butterscotch topping that hardened instantly into a crunchy shell. Partly because of the unfamiliarity of its product, partly because it was closer to high school than was Sawyer's, Zesto enjoyed an immediate rush of business while its more established neighbor bravely maintained that competition was healthy for everyone. But Zesto had no place to sit and talk, only a window where you walked up to order your ice cream. Within a few days, inevitably, the novelty wore off; and the newcomer's popularity subsided to a slow, steady level as the students noisily returned to crowd the booths at Sawyer & Moore, business as usual.

A Great Store
In a Great City

*Sawyer & Moore*
INCORPORATED

1014 West Main St.
*"Durham's Predominating Store"*

*Advertisement in Durham Centennial program, 1953.*

Each year my parents and I went away for a few days during the summer. Once we went to Nags Head, where the beach was nearly empty but for a few frame houses on stilts; we rubbed sweet-smelling Gaby suntan lotion on our faces and shoulders each time we went out into the sun, and my father swam his gentle sidestroke and took me out where the sea was calm, to ride the waves before they crashed onto the shore. A few years later we visited Natural Bridge and Lynchburg, where we stayed with cousins and I was assigned a room of my own, a charming, oddly-shaped, upstairs niche; unable to sleep during that oppressively hot summer night, in desperation I finally got up and pretended I was Heidi, sitting by the window and gazing at the street below. In Richmond we rode our first escalator; in Washington we saw *The Wizard of Oz*, which left me with a penchant for singing "Over the Rainbow" in a voice I hoped sounded like Judy Garland's. Each August my mother and I went to spend a week at my grandfather's farm, where I ran quickly out of books to read, though usually I did succeed in making friends with a cat or two before the week ended; sometimes we walked up to Little River Church to explore the

96

old cemetery where my great-grandparents were buried, and at least once during the week we drove to nearby Hillsborough, where I gratefully drank at an oasis of books in the tiny library next to the Presbyterian Church while my mother and my grandfather shopped and visited in the grocery nearby. And one summer I went home with a friend after church to spend a much-anticipated few days on her family's farm a few miles north of Durham: "Be smart," my father had reminded me (meaning Be agreeable, pleasant, helpful, mannerly) as he always did when I left the house to visit someone, and I tried; but though the farm was beautiful and I dearly loved my friend I was sharply, painfully homesick, and when her mother hospitably urged me to stay longer I was polite but firm in my refusal.

And once each summer my mother and I traveled twenty-five miles southeast to spend a day in Raleigh. From our house we took an early bus downtown to the Mission-styled Union Station behind the courthouse, bought one-way tickets to Raleigh (thirty-five cents for my mother, fifteen for me) and left at 9:15. The train took us through farms and countryside

*Postcard view of Union Station, ca. 1907.*

97

for about forty minutes before pulling into Raleigh's station; from the station we walked up busy Fayetteville Street, past Montgomery Ward and the Ambassador Theatre, to the Hall

FAYETTEVILLE STREET, RALEIGH, N. C.—47

*Postcard view of Raleigh's Fayetteville Street, ca. 1945.*

of History. There we scrutinized uniforms and weapons from all the wars to which North Carolina had sent soldiers; inspected arrowheads and Indian pottery; puzzled over the fate of tiny Virginia Dare. After leaving the Hall of History we visited the Ladies' Room at the Sir Walter Hotel (the Sir Walter, rather than the Capitol, was said to be the center of North Carolina's government) before going to Woolworth's for lunch; early in the afternoon we walked back to the State Museum in the old granite Agricultural Building to admire the mounted animals and the collections of insects, shells, and rocks. Always we ended the day by stopping by the Capitol, a domed, classically-styled nineteenth-century building that wore its years with grace and stood serenely in the middle of Capitol Square, a grassy city block filled with trees, shrubbery, and statues: tallest, most imposing of all stood the Confederate Monument, facing

*Postcard view of State Capitol, Raleigh, ca. 1923.*

Salisbury Street and towering some seventy feet into the air. On Capitol Square we joined other tourists in feeding the pigeons with peanuts that we bought from the vendor for ten cents a bag, though if we'd thought to supply ourselves beforehand with a bag of cracked corn from Stone Bros. or Barnes Supply, the peanut-weary pigeons ignored everyone else to flock around us. By late afternoon we were tired, and it was time to head for the Trailways station to catch a bus back to Durham, and then a Duke Power bus home.

Nothing ever changed on our trips to Raleigh; each time we went to the same places in the same order, so I always knew what was coming next. Nothing changed in the places we went to, either: the rocks, shells, and stuffed animals at the State Museum looked the same the last time I saw them as they did the first. Just once, though, we did walk under the oaks on Blount Street to the Governor's Mansion, an enormous, many-gabled Queen Anne dwelling of red brick and sandstone that my mother said had been built before she was born. Our timid

99

*Postcard view of Governor's Mansion, Raleigh, ca. 1907.*

ring brought forth a pleasant-faced housekeeper who explained regretfully that no tours of the Mansion were scheduled that day; but when my mother murmured that we'd come all the way from Durham, the housekeeper kindly offered to let us look inside a few of the rooms. We walked around on tiptoe and stayed only a few minutes, not wanting, as my mother pointed out, to wear out our welcome; but we did get a glimpse of the high ceilings and elaborate moldings, the ornate mirrors and patterned rugs that filled the reception parlors. Beautiful, we agreed in voices that were suitably hushed. But really, when you got right down to it, not a bit nicer than the Washington Duke Hotel at home.

\* \* \* \* \*

Even before Lakewood Park closed during the 1930's, construction of a new swimming pool had begun on the acreage northeast of town that Brodie Duke had given to the city. A project of the Federal Emergency Relief Administration, Duke

Park Pool was formally transferred into Durham's possession on the evening of 1 August 1934: Mayor Will Carr accepted the facility on behalf of the city, after which former Olympic champion Helen Wainwright Stelling dazzled spectators with her swimming and diving demonstration. The *Herald* later reported that at a business luncheon the following day Mrs. Stelling had delighted members of the Durham Lions' Club by gracefully describing the pool as "one of the finest I have ever seen."

During the summers that followed Duke Park Pool opened its gates nearly every day, closing only during thunderstorms or (rarely, though for weeks at a time) when a polio epidemic raged; and if I didn't go to the Children's Museum or the library, I begged my mother to take me to the pool. When I was little we went to the small, shallow, fenced-in baby pool, but my sixth birthday made me an adult for Duke Park's purposes, and then I graduated to the "big pool" a few hundred feet away. Sometimes Betty Ellington met me at the chlorine-scented bathhouse where we paid nine cents each for admission, received in return a wire basket in which to check our shorts, shirts, and sandals, and shared a wooden booth for changing into our one-piece shirred Latex bathing suits and matching rubber caps. (Robbins was advertising the "Stunner," a two-piece style that dipped revealingly an inch below the navel, but with the stern caution that the suit was intended to be worn only in private; and in fact everyone we saw at the pool was dressed much as we were.) Most of the time, though, I went swimming alone while my mother sat and read in the bleachers above the pool — "swimming" being a generous assessment of what I did, which consisted chiefly of standing in chest-deep water, peering around nearsightedly to see whether I recognized anyone, and doing deep knee bends to make the water come up to my neck. When I did go all the way underwater for a few seconds, it was only after careful preparation — closing my eyes, taking a very deep breath, and pinching my nostrils tightly shut. (For a few days I plugged my ears with my little fingers while pinching my nostrils shut with my thumbs, but that soon came to be too much trouble.)

After watching me spend happy but non-productive afternoons in the pool for a summer or two, my mother decided swimming lessons were in order. Accordingly, she enrolled me in the park's next Learn To Swim course; and on the following Monday morning, together with a dozen other eager learners, I reported punctually and expectantly at the shallow end of the pool for the first class. After checking us off on his list, a bored lifeguard informed us that on hearing our names called we were to cross the pool as best we could. When he began reading out names, a couple of boys plunged in to kick and splash energetically across, carefully holding their heads above water; most of the others in the class met the challenge more sedately, doing Dead Man's Floats with an occasional weak kick or dog paddle to add velocity. On hearing my own name called, I eyed the water warily for a few seconds, summoned my dignity, and began walking cautiously across the pool. Now definitely annoyed, the lifeguard singled me out, along with another girl, for Special Help; and while the others received some rudimentary instruction in breathing and kicking, she and I stood attentively and silently against the edge of the pool. I wondered how long it had taken the Nereidians to learn to swim. Occasionally my companion and I held on with both hands to the trough below the outside edge and kicked vigorously, hoping thereby to appear energetic, even sporty. No one noticed.

When the lifeguard returned to us, which he did with marked reluctance, he explained logically and not unkindly that before he could teach us to swim, we must accustom ourselves to putting our heads under water. We were, in fact, to do so right away. His suggestion lacked appeal, and I stood mutely regarding the water for several seconds, hoping vaguely that either the entire situation would miraculously disappear, or the lifeguard would somehow comprehend my fear and find another, gentler method of instruction. While I hesitated, one of the boys in the class tried to speed things up by pushing me roughly underwater. Caught by surprise and terrified as well, I struggled back to the surface, choking, sputtering, and unable to breathe. The lifeguard, doubtless thinking that was plenty for the first day, mercifully ignored me for the remainder of the lesson; and after my mother had taken me home I indignantly refused to return to the class the following day, or indeed ever again.

Thereupon I determined to learn to swim at my own speed. Beginning with daily sessions of bravely immersing my face in our water-filled bathroom lavatory, over the next few summers I progressed by slow, careful degrees into finally going (voluntarily) under water at the pool. From that point I learned to hold my breath in order to float and kick for a few seconds, but I was incapable of summoning the coordination that would enable me to float, kick, breathe, and move my arms all at once. All that kept me going was Esther Williams: I longed to look as shapely and gorgeous as she did in a succession of stunning bathing suits (though I realized her glamorous gold lamé creations would probably never show up in the Girls' Department at Belk's); I yearned to swim and dive with her easy grace and especially to be lifted, standing, atop a twenty-foot-high fountain. Most of all, though, I envied her gracious underwater smile. While I sincerely wanted to learn to swim, in truth I was much more eager to learn to smile underwater, though who I thought would ever be down there to appreciate the accomplishment, I have no idea.

Over and over I held my breath, propelled myself firmly down to the bottom of the pool, and parted my lips in what I hoped was a dazzling smile, only to choke instantly and race wildly back to the surface for air. Every time I went to the pool I kept trying, to the astonishment and alarm of those around me, but a few weeks into each summer my efforts began to seem futile, and I resumed practicing my basic float-and-kick across the pool. (It was during one of those times that I began to dream nearly every night of discovering happily that a singular gift had been bestowed on me: as long as I inhaled slowly and with deliberate care, I could breathe underwater. No longer for me the struggle to roll my head out of the water at a certain point in my stroke, breathe in exactly the right amount of air, and exhale it at just the proper rate of speed during the following stroke; I could stay underwater indefinitely and tirelessly, breathing in a slow, casual, relaxed fashion, and doing a smooth, perfect stroke and kick that carried me effortlessly the length of the pool in no time at all.)

The eagerly-awaited highlight of Duke Park's summer season came in August, when a cheering, appreciative crowd of several thousand gathered to watch the annual water pageant, a fast-paced show that offered a brass band together with skilled divers and swimmers performing in straight and comic acts. Clowns lost their clothes in mid-air, or went into the pool in flames, or rode a bicycle into the water in a spectacular but ineffective attempt at saving a drowning man (the victim was eventually pulled to safety by a businesslike three-year-old). Girls wearing seal costumes balanced balls on their noses while presenting a precision swimming act, and champion divers performed double gainers and jackknifes that made us gasp.

Every year the crowd left the pageant marveling at the performers' skill. I left it thinking that next year I really would learn to coordinate my motions so I could swim across the pool, and I would *definitely* learn to smile like Esther Williams. Sadly, my underwater smile progressed not at all; but eventually I did reach a point at which I could dive off the low board and swim hurriedly for the side of the pool. My form, though, remained inefficient and awkward. Years later when I registered for my first semester at Duke, an adviser informed me that I would have to pass the swimming test, or else take swimming in Phys. Ed. Terrified by the prospect of damaging my budding social prospects by having to attend a semester's classes with wet hair, I reported that afternoon to the women's gym. There, after trying vainly to maintain my dignity in the semi-nude state required for my Posture Picture, I apprehensively donned my ruffled pink-checked-gingham bathing suit (Shirred For Bosom Interest), mentally girded for action, and marched toward the pool. The instructor, a brisk, muscular woman clad in a conservative navy blue maillot and wearing a whistle on a lanyard, surveyed me gloomily before indicating that I could go ahead whenever I liked. After carefully descending the steps into the shallow end of the pool, I proceeded noisily to splash, kick, and flounder my way to the other end. Making a determined lunge for the side as land hove into view, I gasped for breath, tried to seem poised, and looked expectantly up at the instructor, who gazed at the wall. A short silence followed. At last she pointed out irritably, "You really *should* take swimming."

I concurred agreeably, and inquired, "Do I pass?"

She looked depressed. "I guess so." I clambered gracelessly out of the water, dressed, raced back over to Registration, and signed up for Archery, Golf, and Ballroom Dance before she could change her mind.

It was probably my last chance to learn to smile underwater, and I missed it.

*Prais'd be the fathomless universe,*
*For life and joy, and for objects*
*and knowledge curious....*

— Walt Whitman

CHAPTER 4

# Knowledge Curious

At 707 South Duke Street, between Parker Street and Morehead Avenue and just a block south of the yellow-beige Gothic Revival buildings of the Duke Memorial Methodist Church, stood the rambling, two-storied, white frame residence that housed The Twaddell School. The former Vera Carr, Mrs. Twaddell was a native of Durham and a cousin of General Julian S. Carr; she had begun her study of music as a child of seven and had graduated from Durham's high school on Morris Street before continuing her education at Trinity College. There she joined the Athenian Literary Society and the Parthenon Club, and in 1920 she graduated Phi Beta Kappa and *magna cum laude*. Her senior yearbook caption noted approvingly,

> Vera might ride on her own name, but she doesn't need to take the crips...Music charms her and soothes her during her many labors.
> "And a night shall be filled
>   With music,
> And the cares that infest the day
>   Shall fold their tents like the Arabs
>   As they silently steal away."

During the next sixty-five years Vera Carr Twaddell would share her love of music with more than ten thousand students, who spanned three generations.

109

Following her graduation from Trinity and postgraduate study at the Louisville Conservatory, Vera Carr accepted a position teaching music in the county schools, while continuing also to teach privately as she had begun to do while still enrolled at the College. Her talents quickly attracted the attention of her employers, and within five years she had become Durham County's Supervisor of Music. By then twice-widowed William P. Twaddell had moved from Philadelphia to become director of music in the Durham city schools, as well as at the First Presbyterian Church. With his arrival the community gained a man of exceptional energy and enthusiasm; and less than a year later, on 22 March 1925, Mr. Twaddell's newly-established Durham Children's Choir School presented its first public performance. Participating were sixty children, all of them between nine and twelve years of age, who had practiced twice weekly since January. The *Durham Sun* mused,

> The community choir will perhaps be a disappointment to some. It won't pay the city any cash dividends or relieve us of our taxes...Those who are too busy counting their pennies and adding to them at public expense will not be able to understand the virtue of singing, even among little children.
>
> But Prof. Twaddell's community choir is training voices which shall gladden Durham's ears for years to come. Singing makes Durham a better place in which to live, lifts a bit of the load of responsibility and care from our individual minds and hearts.

It was never recorded that the new choir was a disappointment to anyone, and the Choir School would continue to perform for some fifteen years.

In 1927 Professor Twaddell and Miss Carr were united in marriage. Though the groom was some twenty years older than his vivacious bride, the couple's musical and teaching gifts would harmonize to influence Durham's cultural life for years to come. With no offspring of their own, the two devoted their lives to educating children and young adults who displayed a talent for music; at one time virtually every young musician in town had studied with one or both of the Twaddells. Though in 1933 Mrs. Twaddell resigned her position as county music supervisor in order to open the Twaddell Kindergarten and First Grade (Superior Methods for Superior Children) the following year, Mr. Twaddell continued until the late 1940's as music director for both the First Presbyterian Church and the city schools. Under his dedicated and gifted direction, Durham's high school chorus won the state choral contest with such monotonous regularity that for a while it was barred from competition.

In 1949, only a short time after his retirement, Mr. Twaddell died. A young people's choir sang at his funeral; and the *Herald*'s editorial tribute a few days later observed that he had "dominated choral music in Durham for twenty-five years."


By the time I entered Mrs. Twaddell's in 1943, the school was already nine years old. Since I knew how to read, after a day or two it was decided that I should skip first grade and join the second and third graders, who met cozily together around a table for eight. There we learned about Virginia Dare and the Lost Colony, and stenciled blue and green flower designs on yellow washcloths for our mothers; once or twice a week several of us also went to the front parlor to study piano with either Mr. or Mrs. Twaddell, at fifty cents per lesson. During recess we played in the large back yard that was carpeted with pine needles and shaded by oaks. I admired dark-haired Marjorie Wall, circled warily around pretty, confident Annette Howell, and flirted with Daryl Manley, who repaid my interest by tying me to a tree. One of the teachers scolded him crossly, but it was almost worth it to become a captured heroine, spirited and courageous in the face of peril.

Our teacher was Mrs. Moore, a goodhumored and patient

woman who taught us that the "t" in "often" was always silent, and who saw to it that we formed precise letters, did neat number work, and practiced line after line of overlapping loops and circles that would presumably enable us to produce rounded, even penmanship. For our class project we meticulously printed eight polite, identically worded requests to Philadelphia's Old Flag House and then waited breathlessly for a week, at the end of which the mailman delivered a package that contained for each of us a small, silken reproduction of the Betsy Ross flag. Our Natural Method Readers informed us about the sad fate of beautiful young Echo; about David's bravery and Goliath's fall; about King Midas and his greed. Best of all, though, was the story of May Blossom, the lovely maiden only one inch tall who escaped marriage to a rich old mole by riding far away on a swallow's back: in a land where the sun always shone, she became queen of all the fairies and lived happily ever after.

We learned that North Carolina was the Old North State, the dogwood our state flower, the cardinal our state bird, and we ourselves Tar Heels and proud to be so. We memorized our state song, which petitioned Heaven to shower its blessings on North Carolina, and ended with our vow to Cherish, Protect, and Defend Her. Mrs. Twaddell took this opportunity to stress the proper pronunciation of "Carolina," with all four syllables clearly intact: under no circumstances were we to slip into the careless vulgarity of "Ca-*lina*." Neither were we to refer to the state as "Carolina" alone, but by its full name. No true North Carolinians would ever fall into such error, Mrs. Twaddell assured us, only persons from other states who — as they knew no better — were not to be condemned, but pitied. *Yankees,* someone whispered.

Mrs. Twaddell taught all of us girls to curtsey. "Probably you won't need to curtsey very often, young ladies, but when you do it's important to know how." As it turned out, several of us needed to know how the very next spring, for our May program. Mrs. Twaddell borrowed the Durham High Auditorium for the evening, and Betsy Crutchfield, Earlene Poole, and Betty Love played Queen's Ladies for the Rumpelstiltskin skit; Janet Sue Couch and Lucy Lanning were Noble Ladies at Cinderella's Ball; I was Martha Washington in a costume of my mother's devising, an exquisite long poplin dress with ruffled sleeves and underskirt. The program's grand finale consisted of a minuet in which John Lance Perry played George Washington, Tony Brannon was Christopher Columbus, and Anne Marie Rogers portrayed Betsy Ross. Pointing our toes, taking neat, precise steps in our Colonial costumes, we girls contentedly thought ourselves graceful beyond belief. Not one of us failed to curtsey just as Mrs. Twaddell had taught us.

The Twaddell School continued for over thirty years, until Mrs. Twaddell closed it in 1966; soon afterwards Urban Renewal and an expressway altered the face of South Duke Street, and now even the buildings that housed the school are gone. But eighteen years after the closing, Mrs. Twaddell explained to a visitor that of course she was still teaching piano, though naturally she didn't take as many students as she had in the past. The visitor marveled: how many persons she'd taught, how much she'd accomplished. Reflecting, Mrs.

---

## 𝕿𝖜𝖆𝖉𝖉𝖊𝖑𝖑 𝕾𝖈𝖍𝖔𝖔𝖑

TELEPHONE 3-7061     707 SOUTH DUKE STREET

DURHAM, N. C.

---

*Twaddell School letterhead.*

Twaddell replied, "We all have to do our best. And yes, I really do think I've done everything I could.

"I've done my best."

\* \* \* \* \*

During the spring of 1916 construction began on a new "grammar" school, to be located on Watts Street between Dacian and Urban Avenues; this would be the first public school in Trinity Park, then a growing young suburb on the northwest edge of town. Since the building hadn't been completed when school opened in September, the children who had been newly zoned to go there attended their former schools, Morehead and Fuller and North Durham, for the first few weeks of class. Under the direction of Jean Williams as Principal, Watts Street School opened on Monday, 2 October 1916; on the previous day the *Morning Herald* had hailed the new facility with praise:

> The equipment of the Watts Street building will be the most modern available, and will compare favorably with that of the most recent school buildings of northern cities. The front part of the building is at present being graded and when finished will add greatly to the attractiveness of the place. Cement walks will be laid in the near future, while grass and flower beds will make the ground one of unusual artistic qualities.

A week later another, slightly cautionary, note appeared:

> The playground is the most spacious of all the schools and with the removal of a few stumps, baseball and other athletic games can be played without interfering with the other pupils on the ground at the same time.

During the school's first ten years enrollment increased steadily (by 1923 the six grades showed a total of 110 boys and 109 girls), and in 1927 new classrooms and a gymnasium were added; a new furnace room was built also, while the old furnace room was transformed into a cafeteria.

At the time of original construction it had been proposed that the school be named for George Washington Watts, who then sat on the School Board, and who several years before had given Watts Hospital to the city. But Watts objected to this proposal so strenuously that the idea was dropped, and the new facility became Watts Street School instead. Several years after Watts's death, though, the idea of naming the school in his honor reappeared, and on 1 February 1929 the School Board acted. The *Durham Morning Herald* duly reported,

> In recognition of the services of George W. Watts, former chairman of the board of education, to the cause of public instruction in Durham, it was voted to change the name of the Watts Street School to the George Watts School.

But old habits die hard, and to most Durhamites "Watts Street School" has remained just that for seventy years, despite the change.

The school was only a few years old in 1922 when Lorraine Iseley Pridgen arrived in town to make Durham her home; though her arrival caused little stir at the time, its consequent influence on Watts Street School, its faculty, and three generations of students (and their parents) would be profound. Lorraine Pridgen was a poised, self-disciplined, conscientious young woman who had graduated from Trinity College in 1918, having first completed her practice teaching at Watts Street School under the supervision of one of the College's best known educators, Dr. Eugene C. Brooks; she had then taught in Roanoke Rapids and Lexington for several years before returning to Durham. On her arrival she began work at Trinity on a Master's degree in education; as part of her course work she went to observe at Watts Street, where by then Lily Nelson Jones had become principal. When one of the other teachers contracted scarlet fever, Mrs. Pridgen taught in her stead. Soon afterward she accepted a permanent position as a teacher of geography and nature studies (the city schools had just instituted the platoon system of instruction, which provided a different teacher for each field of study).

Mrs. Pridgen had taught geography at Watts Street for over two decades when the schools dropped the platoon structure to return to the traditional system; after the change she taught sixth grade for a year before, in 1945, being named principal of the school. She would hold that position for the next seventeen years, toward the end of which time she would oversee the education of several grandchildren of her early students, and would welcome one of her former pupils, by then a Duke graduate, on her return to Watts Street School as a teacher. By the time Mrs. Pridgen retired in 1962, she would have served as an educator for forty-five years.

By anyone's lights, she was exceptional. Upon her retirement, a *Herald* article quoted one of her former students as remarking,

> The children know exactly what they can expect of Mrs. Pridgen when they either do their duty or fail to do it. She's their security in an insecure world.

Though she was never known to have treated a child unfairly or unkindly, only a very intrepid, indeed reckless, young person would have had the temerity to defy or disobey Mrs. Pridgen; her disapproval, though, was vastly more bearable than was her sorrowful disappointment in a child who had failed to live up to her expectations. Mothers, though secretly even more daunted than were their children by the prospect of a conference with her (they suddenly became uncomfortably conscious of their grammar, and worried about whether skirts were the proper length), were treated kindly and courteously, as serious partners in the challenging work of shaping occasionally resistant clay into responsible, polite, conscientious citizens of tomorrow. (Throughout her years as principal, Mrs. Pridgen maintained a dignified distance from PTA meetings, diplomatically informing her students' parents that because she trusted them and knew they had the best interests of the school and its children at heart, she preferred allowing them to discuss business in private.)

If Mrs. Pridgen's standards for her children were high, she demanded the best from her teachers as well. Under her aegis the school's faculty set a standard of excellence: such teachers as Elizabeth Grey won statewide recognition, and *Watts Hi-Lights* consistently received awards that took note of its standing as one of the best school newspapers in the city. For seventeen years Watts Street School had the rare good fortune of being managed by a leader who was unswerving in her devotion to discipline, order, and the well-being of the children in her care. Those who attended the school during her era believe that the notion of women's unfitness for positions of command belongs solely to those who never knew Mrs. Pridgen.

Mrs. Twaddell's had provided a warm, sheltered introduction to learning; but Watts Street, I decided, was a *real* school. Constructed of red brick, the building had two front entrances — one for boys, one for girls — and stood exactly two and a half stories high (the "half" was the basement cafeteria, whose windows near the ceiling opened just above ground level on the front of the school: when we looked up from our meat loaf and boiled carrots to gaze outside, we could see only the sky, with an occasional tree top for variety). The classrooms were much alike: one end was lined with half a dozen blackboard sections, each of which pulled open to reveal a cloakroom filled with galoshes, raincoats, and booksacks. Pull-down maps hung close to the teacher's desk, and letters in smooth, cursive script marched ovally around the room, just above the blackboard, for us to copy. Underneath our desks hung handy compartments for books we weren't using; at the top of the desk's writing surface, a conveniently hollowed-out impression held a pencil. (The protruding inkwell at the side was long unused and slightly rusty, since Watts Street's students had years before adopted modern fountain pens that could be filled with ink, rather than dipped.)

The second floor held an auditorium with a real stage, which remained concealed behind heavy moss-green velvet curtains when it wasn't in use; facing the stage stood some twenty rows of fold-down wooden seats. The windows were hidden behind sedate velvet curtains that matched the one on stage; the wooden floor was polished to a shine; a North Carolina flag stood to our left of the stage, a United States flag to the right. Institutional green covered all — classrooms, cafeteria, auditorium, and halls — presumably on the premise that since pupils were so easily stimulated into unruly disorder, they must be continuously soothed, quieted, and disciplined into scholarly pursuits.

Miss Cole, my new teacher, was young and kind, but the notion of entering a classroom filled with twenty-five strangers left me faint with fear; and so for my first two weeks at Watts Street my mother accompanied me every day, sitting patiently at the back of the room and listening to fourth-grade spelling, geography, and arithmetic, until I was adjudged to have made a successful transition from Mrs. Twaddell's into the wider world of public school. When I finally mustered courage enough to lift my eyes and speak to my classmates, I was spellbound to discover that the girl in front of me, Evelyn Stocker, was *Swiss*. Instantly she took on an exotic luster in my eyes, and we became friends. Evelyn was artless, happy-tempered, and eager as a puppy; her pretty, olive-complexioned features were framed by dark, straight hair that she wore pinned back by two barrettes, and when she sat down, invariably she put both hands primly behind her to smooth her skirt. I thought this a charming mannerism, doubtless Swiss in origin, and promptly began to imitate it, but no one noticed. Despite her foreign origins, Evelyn's clothes looked disappointingly conventional, much like garments any American girls might wear and not at all like the pictures in my copy of *Heidi*, and it soon developed that she didn't speak Swiss either, only German. But during the summers she and her family returned to Switzerland, and eventually I received several suitably foreign-looking post cards that offered breathtaking mountain views, splendidly illustrated stamps, a message section filled with Evelyn's tiny, precise handwriting, and my name and address, neatly printed, with a significant "U.S.A." at the end. (I pointed that out to the postman, to make sure he noticed.)

Watts Street informed its pupils about a number of things, some of them not in the curriculum. Geography taught us about the Tigris, the Euphrates, and the Nile; about coolies, silkworms, and tea; about dikes, and canals, and the Zuider Zee. (As well as being filled with useful if occasionally drab facts, the geography book was tall and wide, convenient for concealing an illegal Nancy Drew in front.) In Art we expressed our budding creativity in watercolors, meanwhile tolerantly over-looking periodic damp outbursts from our untidy, excitable teacher, who believed sixth-graders existed solely to blight her life. That year the girls were assembled to view a cheery, animated film that — just as worldly-wise Martha Hansen had predicted — concerned Minnustration. A few days later one of the boys, eager to contribute information of his own now that the subject had been broached, smuggled out to recess a contraband *National Geographic* in which an article on Samoa offered several riveting pictures of native women, bare to the waist. The playground population was mesmerized, but this sensational disclosure was short-lived. Ever alert to the ways of sixth-grade boys, Miss Brown quickly spotted the unusual excitement, nabbed the offender, and whisked him off to the office, where he spent the remainder of the day huddled miserably under the cool, measured gaze of Mrs. Pridgen.

Mostly, though, school days proceeded quietly. Miss Cole taught us to play "An English Country Garden" on red plastic flutes, and each day after Tiptoe Recess we went to Music, where we learned to sing "Beautiful Dreamer," "Funiculi, Funicula," and "Stouthearted Men." We read our *Weekly Readers* and *Watts Hi-Lights,* spent several hours practicing the proper way to open a book, and — though mostly she entertained the first and second-graders — sometimes we heard the Story Lady, Jane Wilson. Only once in a while did we have real drama, as when — for reasons that remained ever cloudy — an overwrought fourth-grader used a sharp pencil to stab the girl sitting in front of her; happily, the stabbee suffered only a minor flesh wound, but teachers and students alike discussed the incident in low, confidential whispers for the rest of the day.

Frequently we filed into the auditorium for special programs, bringing canned offerings and singing "We Gather Together" for Thanksgiving, hearing Velma Brown recite "Little Orphant Annie" at Hallowe'en. When a group of American Indians presented a selection of sacred songs, we applauded enthusiastically; after the performers had left, Mrs. Pridgen seized the opportunity to deliver a brief but firm rebuke, pointing out that one never, never applauded sacred music, the only proper tribute to which was reverent silence. (To this day, hearing sacred music greeted by applause causes former Watts Street students to squirm in their seats while glancing uneasily around, perhaps unconsciously expecting Mrs. Pridgen to appear and administer the appropriate correction.)

Recess offered several options. One year a passion for horses gripped several of the girls, who under Sally Russell's tutelage took to spending their free time cantering, whinnying, and galloping around the playground. The sixth grade members of Mrs. Zollicoffer's Girl Scout Troop regaled the rest of us with the interminable adventures of a child whose name began with

"Sticky-sticky stombone" and ended ten seconds later; happily, though, after a week or two Sticky's lengthy deeds lost their charm even to the storytellers, and we were spared. Sometimes we practiced the tango and foxtrot steps Mr. Satterfield had taught in his dance class the week before. Blond, petite Grace Hess joined us for fifth grade, so dazzling us with her skill at turning cartwheels and handsprings that we nearly killed ourselves trying to do likewise. We played dodge ball, and kick ball as well, though since Miss Cole had discovered my nearsightedness and sent home a note to my mother that resulted in my spending a day at McPherson's Hospital, whence I emerged wearing thick, gold-rimmed glasses, I'd lost my fondness for games that involved the approach of a fast ball. Just once, though, after the others had gone Out, I stayed in the ring to dodge ten throws by Kay Penny and Margaret Hannah, the best athletes of us all, while my classmates stood by and cheered — loud, satisfying cheers that rang triumphantly in my ears long afterward. I trailed clouds of glory for a week.

For most of us, sixth-grade graduation was the grandest occasion life had offered thus far. The girls composed a vision of modest innocence in white: a few appeared in batiste, dotted swiss, or piqué, but most of us opted for cap-sleeved organdy, occasionally with ruffles, which we believed to convey an impression of suitably fragile elegance. Carolyn Hart looked daringly mature in white sandals and nylon stockings; Helen Baker (an artist, and therefore expected to differ from the norm) was similarly attired; but the rest of us wore our usual Sunday white socks and patent leather Mary Janes. Hair flowed, mostly: Nancy Sanders and Kay Penny wore neat white bandeaux to hold back their long, dark locks; Jean Gerard added drama by wearing a white flower in her flaxen-blond, Alice-in-Wonderland tresses; Evelyn Stocker, her rich beauty by then becoming obvious, let her deep brown ringlets fall freely to her shoulders. The boys, on the other hand, all sported fresh haircuts — a trifle too short — and looked unnaturally stiff, scrubbed, and polished in white shirt and trousers, dark sport coats and ties. At the auditorium door we lined up in boy-girl pairs, beginning from the shortest (Benny Roberts and myself) in front, and continuing through the class to the tallest (Benny Kaplan and Mary Grace Maupin) in back. Mrs. Pridgen, a martinet in tailored pink linen, inspected her company — straightening a tie here, retying a sash there, adjusting a hem that had been turned up in the general breathless excitement of the morning. Then the pianist began to play "Onward, Christian Soldiers," and our parents stood in the auditorium, and it was time to march — straight, proud, and eyes forward — down the aisle.

Each year the Lily Nelson Jones Cup was presented to that sixth-grade girl who was voted Outstanding by the faculty. For weeks we'd debated who would win this year's award; but since several girls seemed likely candidates, the cup's disposition remained in doubt. The boys' award, the Cannon Cup, presented no such difficulty, for everyone knew it could go to only one person — bright, affable, hardworking Safety-Patroler Rex Morgan. (Rex, though modestly noncommittal, thought so too.) But when the moment came for presenting the two honors, a double surprise awaited us. Miss Jones, the school's beloved and now aged former principal, awarded the silver cup named for her to *two* girls, Betsy Lyon and Nancy Sanders, the first such double award in the school's history. This was surprising, but agreeable. The bombshell came a few minutes later: the Cannon Cup went not to Rex as we'd expected, but to Jonathan Wood, a brilliant but quiet student whose name elicited an unrehearsed and clearly audible gasp of surprise from the Class of 1948. Since he had a part in the program, Rex was sitting on the stage facing classmates, teachers, and parents; though momentarily stunned by the shock of hearing his classmate's name instead of his own, he quickly regained his composure and contrived to appear genial, even congratulatory, while the cup's recipient walked onstage.

Jonathan accepted his prize, shook hands with Mrs. Pridgen, and returned to his seat as the audience applauded; the sixth-graders' eyes, though, remained not on the winner but on Rex. Mentally we surrounded him with a protective circle, wishfully remolding the awarding of the cup. Rex looked pleasant, composed, and calm. His courage under fire escaped no one's notice.

We marched up front to accept our diplomas; listened to our valedictory address; sang for the last time about straw hats, and fishing poles, and June. When the exercises had ended and we started to leave, Margot Regen said she thought she'd seen tears in Mrs. Pridgen's eyes when we began our march down the aisle; but no one knew for sure.

* * * * *

In 1947, soon after her twin daughters had graduated from Watts Street School, Frances Gray Patton published a short story that told of a geography teacher, a veteran of several decades of teaching, who was firm in authority and strict in discipline, but unfaltering in her love for the children in her care. Six years later Mrs. Patton's *Good Morning, Miss Dove*, a full-length novel inspired by the earlier story, became one of the best-selling books of the decade. Across the country readers were captivated by the redoubtable Miss Dove; Durhamites, delighted at such an accomplishment by one of their number, likewise hastened to read the book. Those who knew Watts Street School and its principal quickly concluded that, allowing for a few minor liberties with facts, Miss Dove was an affectionate portrayal of Mrs. Pridgen. Whether this was in fact the case remains unknown, but Mrs. Patton characterized her geography teacher with precision and vigor:

Miss Dove was a certainty. She would be today what she had been yesterday and would be tomorrow.

And:

She had an extra quality as compelling as personal charm...that captured the imagination. She gave off a sort of effulgence of awe and terror. But the terror did not paralyze. It was terror that caused children to flex their moral muscles and to dream of enduring, without a whimper, prolonged ordeals of privation and fatigue.

And:

Her love flowed out to those children — to those with their pen points poised above their paper and to those in the far places she had once helped them locate on the map. It did not flow tenderly like a coddling mother's love. It flowed on a fierce rush of hope and pride, the way an old general's heart might follow his men into battle.

And:

Each June some forty-odd little girls and boys — transformed by the magic of organdy ruffles and white duck pants into a group picture of purity — were graduated from Cedar Grove. They went on to the wider world of junior high and, beyond that, to further realms of pleasure and pain. In the course of time they forgot much. They forgot dates and decimals and how to write business letters. But they never forgot Miss Dove.

At Watts Street, they never forgot Mrs. Pridgen.

*Dreams, books, are each a world;*
*and books, we know,*
*Are a substantial world....*

— *William Wordsworth*

# CHAPTER 5
# Dreams, Books

The Children's Museum offered Nature for my teacher, the radio broadcast a world of entertainment; but books were my life. I'd begun reading early, matching up nursery rhymes with pictures and print as my mother read to me; and by the time I was four, she and my father, encouraged by my progress, had bought me an imposing set of *The Book of Knowledge,* bound in textured red leatherette and neatly housed in its own walnut bookcase. Encyclopedias offered all kinds of useful information, it seemed; and one evening soon thereafter my father had his quiet dinner interrupted by an unexpected query as to whether Santa Claus was *really* one's parents. Visibly perturbed, he parried the attack by asking what had prompted the question, whereupon I explained about the disclosure in my *Book of Knowledge.* This was hard to refute. At last he crossly admitted the truth about Santa, cautioning that I was to keep the secret to myself. I agreed, and waited till the next morning to relay the news to Ruth Jernigan, who refused to believe it. During the years that followed we never again mentioned the matter at home, and Santa remained benevolent: amiably overlooking my momentary lapse of faith, he continued to leave a gift under our tree each Christmas Eve until I finished college.

Never again did I learn anything quite so earth-shaking from an encyclopedia; and in fact, as worthy a work as was *The Book of Knowledge,* for pleasure reading I soon found it couldn't hold a candle to *Donald Duck, The Katzenjammer Kids,* and *Blondie.* Soon, too, I became acquainted with the Bobbsey Twins, both sets of them — dark-haired, eight-year-old Nan and Bert, and blond, four-year-old Freddie and Flossie, whom Mr. Bobbsey had affectionately nicknamed Fat Fireman and Fat Fairy. Nan and Bert were extraordinarily mature for their ages, and the whole family was forever going to interesting places — Blueberry Island, or Echo Valley, or Cherry Corners. The Bobbseys' life was tidy and neat: none of them was ever menaced by a dangerous chandelier, or had a drooping bandage that showed in a newspaper picture, or got stung by a honeybee (that stung only because he was mashed between the cupped bare hands of a person who caught him to show off). Apart from dropping in occasionally to call the younger twins by their nicknames, Mr. Bobbsey appeared but rarely; but it was understood that he stayed busy with his lumberyard, there by the shore of Lake Metoka. Only when ruffian Danny Rugg showed up did trouble start; otherwise, calm reigned in Lakeport.

The Bobbsey Twins soon began making regular appearances on birthdays and Christmas, but meanwhile my library had received a major boost with my parents' purchase of another encyclopedia. *The New Wonder World* was lovely to look at: its eleven volumes were bound in several different colors; its pages were thick and glossy; and the front cover of each volume bore a colored miniature suggesting that book's contents. The endpapers fancifully pictured three children looking at an open book as they sat beside a river in which swam half a dozen varieties of fish; across the river stood a fairy princess, Ben Franklin flying his kite, Davy Crockett, a veiled Moslem woman, an elephant and a camel, an Indian charming a snake. A Viking ship shared the river with a steamship, and in the very back of the scene stood a castle on a hilltop.

History, Inventions, and Sports all had their volumes; but I read only the collections of stories and verse — *The Literature Book,* and *Story and Art,* and *The Child in the Home.* In those three volumes dwelt a host of beings, real and mythical, whose very names carried magic, and whose deeds wholly captured my fancy. Little Black Sambo regained his fine clothes, and the young Arthur drew a sword from a stone to win a kingdom; Perseus slew the dreaded Medusa, and Dick Whittington's cat brought him wealth. Rapunzel let down her locks; the Snow-white cow brought Krinka her prince; Alice pursued a Rabbit wearing a waistcoat; the Sleeping Beauty woke to a kiss. Credulous, kindhearted Dr. Primrose encountered the wicked ways of the world; brave Dobbin fought Cuff for mistreating a fellow schoolmate; and the Light Brigade rode into the jaws of Death. Transformations abounded: a frog became a prince; Little Scar Face became beautiful; sooty, grimy Tom the chimney-sweep became a water baby. Verses bore me up into the cherry tree, and where the golden apples grow. The Bible came alive: the walls of Jericho tumbled; Jonathan saved his beloved David from the wrath of Saul; Hannah dedicated her Samuel to the Lord. The young Charles Dickens worked in a blacking factory, and little Florence Nightingale cared tenderly for her sick dolls; Nelly Umbstaetter's whimsical Cloud-Makers and Wind-Gatherers labored busily in full pages of color. And an article on treasure-hunting in one's attic explained how to make wonderful things out of newspapers, paper bags, cardboard boxes, and tinfoil: seldom did I make anything, but I did love reading about it.

(Only once did *The New Wonder World* fail me. When I looked in the *Wonder of Life* volume for an explanation of the mysteries of sex, I found a lengthy though illuminating discussion of reproduction in yeast plants, butterflies, and peas. Concluding this informative essay was an oblique statement that the story ended with a baby in its mother's arms. How one negotiated the quantum leap from butterflies to babies, though, remained obscure.)

It was just a couple of years later, one day during fourth-grade arithmetic class at Watts Street, that Ginny Graham passed me a contraband Nancy Drew mystery and generously offered to lend it. Up till then I'd never even heard of Nancy Drew; but I took the book home that afternoon, and before bedtime had read it through. Thereafter the Bobbsey Twins faded into the background, eclipsed by this new heroine who was golden-haired and lovely, self-assured and well-dressed, and whose father — tall, grey-haired, distinguished-looking Carson Drew — was the leading attorney in River Heights. As if all that weren't enough, Nancy possessed an amazing gift for solving mysteries that baffled slower-witted grownups; and best of all, she was never conceited and never vain, but wore her laurels with becoming modesty and grace.

Her accomplishments were legion. Though at sixteen she appeared to attend no school, and never mentioned planning to enter college, somehow she'd absorbed an amazing variety of information: she read Chaucer with ease, knew and enjoyed Shakespeare, and lucidly explained the etymology of "delphinium." (Her delphiniums took first place in the local flower show.) She also remarked knowledgeably on the peculiarities of Colonial architecture, translated the Swedish inscription on a ring found at the scene of a crime, and formulated a plan that successfully exposed a mail robbery scheme. She filled in efficiently and charmingly as a waitress in a tea room, quickly bringing smiles to the faces of customers who had become disgruntled by their wait for service. A paragon of physical skills, she rode and swam expertly (once, having jumped into a bayou fully clothed, she easily covered

the five hundred yards to the shore); she likewise danced a
perfect minuet, climbed a rose trellis to a second-floor window,
won the River Heights Yacht Club's sailboat race, and at a
moment's notice stepped in to perform a ballet for the Woman's
Club, which had been left in the lurch by its star performer.
Managing somehow to survive endless blows to the head as
well as at least one bolt of lightning, on one memorable occasion
she felled a thug with a well-aimed right to the jaw.

If her mental and physical talents were spectacular, Nancy's
character approached perfection. She helped out with the
crippled children's benefit, kept up "a constant stream of good-
natured banter" with a friend in order to cheer a low-spirited
acquaintance, and — though she spoke forcefully, and
unconsciously assumed leadership in any crowd — never thrust
her opinions upon others. Her apparently instinctive
understanding of human psychology was acute: having easily
persuaded a hitherto reluctant taxi driver to identify a man who
had kidnapped her father, she then extricated the truth from
the kidnapper himself. (The police captain was stunned by her
success.) And when she found two deserving acquaintances low
on funds and virtually without food, she gracefully planned a
feast for which she and her friends bought provisions, sensibly
taking care to include enough staples for at least a week.

The crooks who impinged on Nancy's world were easy to
spot. The men had shifty gazes and raucous laughs, wore loud
clothes, and were "completely lacking in good manners"; their
female accomplices, likewise overdressed, were given to
hysterical screams and baleful glares at the young sleuth when
their thieving schemes were brought to light. Excluding these
unprincipled characters, most of whom either drugged, struck,
or kidnapped her, grownups universally treated Nancy with
respect. Her father asked her opinion whenever he had an
important case, and police inspectors addressed her as "Miss
Drew." On one occasion she and her friends were detained

by policemen who were ignorant of her identity; but when she gave her name the captain and detective exchanged meaningful looks, and thereafter the girls were treated with more courtesy. On hearing Nancy bring her keen mind to bear on the facts of a puzzling case, an astonished police captain observed deferentially that she was a "very clear thinker." Ever logical and sensible, always vivacious and never dull, Nancy was a perfect (and smarter) blend of her two best friends, ultra-feminine Bess Marvin and tomboyish George Fayne. Traveling with her brassbound steamer trunk, breaking up a daring counterfeiting ring, reuniting long-separated twins, skillfully maneuvering her snappy roadster (with rumble seat) — Nancy was my idol. My library grew apace.

Soon after discovering Nancy Drew, I also found out about Judy Bolton. Like Nancy, Judy was the daughter of a successful professional man — a physician — and was courageous, smart, and a whiz at solving mysteries; despite her family's comfortable financial circumstances, though, she remained unpretentious and close to reality, living as she did in a house oddly located on a dividing line between the simple cottages of the mill workers and the grand dwellings of the rich. Living in one of those grand dwellings were the Farringdon-Petts, the wealthiest family in town: their turreted mansion was filled with deep-piled rugs, and their white-aproned black maid fascinated the democratic but inexperienced Judy, who "had never seen a negro except in pictures."

Despite their wealth and a certain colorlessness, Arthur and Lois Farringdon-Pett proved to be kind, down-to-earth, un-spoiled young people who became Judy's faithful friends. In sharp contrast to the Farringdon-Petts stood beautiful, arrogant, golden-haired Lorraine Lee, who disliked Judy intensely and resented her friendship with Lois. Though Arthur longed to marry the young detective, Judy fell inconveniently in love instead with a brilliant but impoverished law student, Peter

Dobbs; ever the diplomat, she succeeded in convincing Arthur that his real love was Lorraine, who thereupon stunned readers by experiencing a sudden change of heart to become Judy's admiring friend. Eventually the two couples married in a double ceremony after which Judy intended to live modestly in a tiny cottage as "plain Mrs. Peter Dobbs" with her new husband and Blackberry, her cat. But she'd failed to reckon with her Destiny, which decreed otherwise: to her readers' delighted relief, mysteries continued to seek her out, and she solved them still.

Nancy Drews and Judy Boltons came my way mostly at Christmastime; comic books were every day. For years I subscribed to *Walt Disney's Comics* and *Looney Tunes and Merrie Melodies,* which arrived each month in the mail (a year's subscription cost only a dollar, so you saved twenty cents on the newsstand price). Other comics, though, I usually bought at either Sawyer & Moore or Walgreen's. I admired the modesty and strength of Superman, but liked the Marvel family best of all: for ten cents I joined the Mary Marvel Club, which provided me with a magic membership card, a secret code finder, and a wooden badge showing Mary in flight, her cape streaming behind. I said "Holy Moley" instead of "Gosh" until people began to look at me oddly; and when I was sure nobody was listening I went around the house pronouncing "Shazam" in a low, firm voice, but nothing ever happened. *Patsy Walker* and *Archie* were fun to read, and sometimes their ads were even better, offering such buys as an exquisitely painted 20" x 30" plastic tablecloth reverently depicting the birth of Christ (only $1.00 plus 25¢ postage and handling), a book on how to write love letters (50¢), and, for only $3.95, a mini-gym just like the one that turned thin, colorless Dateless Dorothy into curvy, fascinating Dazzling Dotty ("But Bill, you shouldn't have kidnapped me from the dance like this! What will Jerry think?" "To heck with Jerry! You're going to marry me! You'll be wearing my ring as soon as the stores open tomorrow! So say 'Yes' fast, Dotty!") I never sent for the mini-gym, which was beyond my means; but about every other month, transfixed by ads that brutally pointed out, "Skinny Girls Don't Have OOMPH!", I begged my mother to let me send ninety-eight cents for a bottle of Numal, guaranteed to add extra alluring pounds that would help bring out those natural eye-catching curves. She said No.

\* \* \* \* \*

Along with books and comics, I had the *Durham Morning Herald*. Since my parents read the newspaper every day, I decided early on that it was for me too, and forthwith began to read it each morning. Or part of it. At that time consciousness remained unraised, and no one had yet begun referring non-discriminatorily to certain pages of the newspaper as Style, Living, Taste, People, or Home; rather, the society editor took the direct approach in addressing her audience, decisively titling her pages The World of Women. Here was the world of love and romance, children and family; of sewing, cooking, and crafts; of weddings and birthdays, and the parties that celebrated them; of feminine beauty, and Society, and Home. (Presumably there was a World of Men too, but it didn't occupy a separate section.)

The *Herald* punctiliously chronicled what took place within that world, and I, an eager initiate, read it all. There were long listings of church circle and Sunday-School class meetings; birth announcements, and pictures of new mothers with their babies; reports on who had the flu, who had just left the hospital, and who had gone to the beach. Seven-year-olds' birthday parties were faithfully recorded right down to the crepe paper streamers, the guest list of fifteen Messrs., entertainment by Wallace the Magician, and the Teddy bear cake accompanied by blocks of vanilla, chocolate, and strawberry ice cream. There were descriptions of club meetings; articles on anniversary, going-away, and welcome-home parties; social columns for Hillsborough, and Roxboro, and Warrenton. And when autumn arrived, it was time for a report on Durham's Little Red Hens, a relaxed group whose membership stayed nearly the same (with infrequent additions), and that bestirred itself to action only for its cheerful annual luncheon, decorated with traditional, carefully-saved red hen figurines and linens to match.

Birthday parties and circle meetings received their due, but the emphasis of the women's section fell most heavily on love, romance, and the family. Angelo Patri offered sober, kind, and reasonable guidance on rearing children (if you had an aloof child, you should love him and leave him alone); Dorothy Dix, never at a loss for a solution, gamely tackled problems ranging from mother-in-law frictions to difficulties with uncles who imbibed too freely at family reunions. (She also counselled on "luring a husband," pointing out pragmatically that in the war between the sexes, a woman's most important offensive weapon was her cooking skill: "It isn't love that drives [men] into matrimony so often as it is hunger.") Daily serialized fiction — *Her Perilous Love, Let Love Go, Kitten In The Woods* — dealt with the life of the heart; James J. Metcalfe's rhymed verses left me bathed in sentiment and awash in tears.

But it was in wedding coverage that the newspaper really shone. It all began with a relatively modest engagement announcement: a 5" x 7" photograph of the bride-to-be accompanied an article that listed names of the affianced couple, their education and places of employment, their parents' names, and the date and place scheduled for the ceremony. After that one leapt into a dizzying round of luncheons, teas, and showers, all described down to the last detail including names of punch-servers, identification of flowers in the honoree's corsage, a guest list indicating each person's kinship to the bride-to-be, and an inventory of the mints, nuts, and chicken salad sandwiches. Had the event been dignified by the presence of one of the newspaper's photographers, the article was accompanied by a picture of the honoree, her mother, and the hostess. And if, in addition to the luncheons and teas, the schedule included a party that numbered males among its guests — a cookout, perhaps — that too was recorded, only in language somewhat more restrained and matter-of-fact than that used for the women's parties.

When an article titled "Plans announced for Smith-Jones Nuptials" appeared, the countdown was on. "Plans," which included a succinct recitation of time and place for the ceremony, together with names of everyone in the wedding party, concluded the prenuptial buildup in print; culmination came soon thereafter, in the form of a suitably impressive wedding article. An account of a society wedding could easily occupy two page-length columns: beginning with the bride's and groom's full names along with those of their parents (and, in cases of exalted social standing, their grandparents), the article then named organist, vocalist, and musical selections before launching into a listing of the entire wedding party. Following the bridal attendants' names came full details of their costumes, from flower bandeaux to dyed-to-match silk shoes; groomsmen were listed likewise, though one brief sentence was considered sufficient for describing their attire.

The account reached its apogee with a rhapsodic, one- or two-paragraph description of the bride's ivory satin gown, train, rose point lace veil, diamond pendant necklace given her by the groom, bouquet of white roses centered with white orchid, and matching silk shoes. This was followed by particulars of the outfits worn by the mothers and grandmothers of the couple — rose and blue crepe gowns, orchid corsages, and dyed-to-match shoes. A rendering of the reception included descriptions of the flowers, names of friends who presided over the bride's book and at the punch bowl, and a brief history of the implement used to cut the wedding cake. Now, on a falling note, came an announcement of the couple's honeymoon plans, followed by a description of the bride's traveling outfit — suit, shoes, hat, and corsage. For anyone who was still reading, the account subsided quietly into a businesslike summary of the bride's and groom's education and present employment, a note as to when and where the bride had made her debut, and a list of out-of-town guests attending the wedding.

Years later a friend of mine became society editor of a newspaper, and then I heard first-hand of the hazards of writing wedding accounts. No newspaper articles were ever scrutinized more meticulously by readers for accuracy and comprehensiveness, and all society editors received occasional irate calls from brides' mothers, complaining of anything from a misspelled name to an inadequately delineated wedding dress. Columnists soon discovered that writing half a dozen heavily descriptive wedding articles each week tended to blur the subtle distinctions between ivory, candlelight, and cream; as the weekend approached, harried writers became glazed, numb, and occasionally profane.

Such exquisitely detailed accounts have long since disappeared. Those that adorn old scrapbooks are quaint remnants of a more leisured time, when recording devices were unavailable or too expensive for most people, and newspaper articles supplied the only thorough record of the occasion when a couple began a life together. And could any visual record ever satisfy so fully? If the groom were less than dashing, if the bride were past her bloom, the articles never told. Instead, they gracefully left such matters to the memory or imagination of the reader, who painted in the colors to please herself. Never mind the amount of the rhetoric, the minuteness of the detail, the number of the lists: with weddings, anything worth doing was worth overdoing. Indeed, a fine excess.

\* \* \* \* \*

When I ran out of books to read, I could always work on my scrapbook. Actually I had several scrapbooks that among them encompassed anything I was likely to want to save, which was nearly everything. Easter, Hallowe'en, Thanksgiving all had their own albums, filled with colored pictures carefully cut out of greeting cards, Sunday-School folders, and magazines. All of John Robert Powers's newspaper hints went straight into a scrapbook titled, like the columns, *Secrets of Charm*. Larger than any of these, my main scrapbook contained all the letters and flower enclosure cards my mother had received when I was born, cards I'd received for each birthday, get-well cards I'd been sent when I fractured my arm, letters from my best friend Grace Hess, my test scores from the Twaddell School, and two ration books; later pages contained a mailing label from the Mary Marvel Club, a post card acknowledging my *Looney Tunes and Merrie Melodies* subscription, and a white feather carefully captioned, "In memory of pigeon feeding, Raleigh, August 13, 1947."

I kept one scrapbook specifically for Uncle Ray's Scrapbook Club, for which I had been issued a Membership Certificate that spelled out club rules: after reading "Uncle Ray's Corner" in the *Herald* each day, I was to clip it from the paper and paste it in the proper section of my scrapbook (Uncle Ray was always good about telling you which section the article should go into); also I was to tell my friends about the Scrapbook Club and encourage them to join. I was to show my scrapbook to my teacher from time to time, requesting advice on how to improve it. And in the event I ever failed to find "Uncle Ray's Corner" in our newspaper I was to write or telephone the editor *immediately*, or else ask my mother or father to call him for me: the editor would be glad, Uncle Ray assured me, to know of my interest in the "Corner." The Science section of my scrapbook contained articles on Eustacian tubes, the planet Pluto, and Japanese beetles; Nature articles discussed ladybugs, centipedes, and blue gum trees; Biography contained pieces on Jenny Lind, Oliver Goldsmith, and Daniel Boone. Secretly I thought Uncle Ray's columns were sometimes a little dull, as he seemed inescapably fixed on the real world of average rainfall and locust trees, and never ventured at all into realms of enchantment; still, his articles were there in the *Herald* just for people my age to enjoy, and usually out of a sense of duty I did read them. And they did make a nice scrapbook.

I loved the collecting and organizing that went into making scrapbooks; but a couple of years after the war had ended I discovered happily that one could collect, organize, *and* help war-torn Europe get back to her feet, by providing some fortunate child with an Overseas Friendship Kit. To assemble a kit you first prevailed on your father to contribute an empty cigar box, and then you begged from your mother a few small necessities to pack inside: needles, pins, and thread; a bar of Swan soap; a pad of note paper with pencil; a package or two of Beech-Nut gum; a book of matches; a washcloth; a package of Chesterfields or Luckies if you had a sample around the house. For toys you included a pair of red or blue yarn dolls, along with an inch-long, multi-colored plastic puzzle dog that could be taken into pieces and then reassembled.

So the recipient could learn something about your home town, you included a couple of local post cards (I liked to send one that had an aerial view of Duke, another that showed the intersection of Main and Corcoran Streets — a nice, clear view of the Geer Building, the Woolworth's awning, and the Eckerd's sign). And, of course, a note including your name, age, address, and a polite request that the recipient write if she knew American. Then, after wrapping the box carefully in brown paper and tying it with strong twine, you labeled it on the outside to indicate for whom it was intended — "For A Little

Girl In Holland," or France, or Belgium as the case might be — and mailed it to one of the Overseas Relief organizations. It did seem unsuitable to be sending cigarettes to a little girl, but the Relief people said they were much wanted, and I assumed the kit's recipient would pass the Chesterfields along to her father, brother, or uncle. Overseas Relief was punctual about gracefully acknowledging my contributions toward rebuilding Europe, and I always longed to hear from the Little Girl In Holland or France so we could correspond; but I never received any letters — in American or otherwise — and I could only hope the parcels had managed to reach their destination.

A few years later, though, I walked into our school library one afternoon to find that Miss Loftin had received several letters from Japanese boys and girls who were hoping to find American pen pals. The letter I chose began,

> Dear my friend,
> How to you do. I have the first my friend in letter. I say the myself a few. I am a Japanese girl 15 years old and Utsunomiya high school.

She and her brother lived with their parents, she continued; she enjoyed volleyball and reading, and she had four close friends. Her name was Masako Shimanuki; and when I replied to her letter, I began a correspondence that brushed my next two years with magic.

Her picture arrived a few weeks later, showing a serious young girl wearing a dark, Western-style school uniform. She wrote on translucent paper, lightly bordered with flowers, and enclosed post cards with colored drawings: a pair of wooden dolls, a snow-covered mountain, a lovely young woman in kimono, a waterfall. In April she wrote, "At my house garden be in bloom of kinds flowers. There are a pansy, a vaolet, a primrose, a camellia.... Now Japan be in bloom the cherry very

very beautiful"; with her note she enclosed a pressed pansy, a violet, and an incredibly thin, fragile leaf. She sent one drawing of a sailboat, another of tall, slender trees; and once she reported happily that she and her classmates had completed their examinations — "very difficult, but now we have the self-possession." For my birthday she sent a small, chubby, porcelain doll, dressed in a bit of red and gold brocade and pulling a minute, exquisitely carved red fish.

Everything she sent was delicate and beautiful; I, frustrated, could find nothing so lovely to send her in return. I did my uninspired best, sending issues of *American Girl* and *Seventeen*, post cards showing Duke Chapel and the Washington Duke Hotel, a Christmas issue of *Ideals*. Always she thanked me gracefully, ending with an apology for her English — "Please excuse if I many mistakes."

We sent packages and wrote letters for two years, until it seemed we ran out of things to say. More and more frequently Masako apologized that she couldn't write much because she was so busy; I, on the other hand, was beginning to daydream about college, and boys. Finally one of us left off writing, and the correspondence ended. But I put the delicately tinted post cards and New Year's greetings into my scrapbook; and in my bookcase stands a happy, gaily-dressed Japanese boy in the middle of a step, pulling behind him a tiny, red, wooden fish.

*When I wake with the blest*
*In the mansions of rest,*
*Will there be any stars in my crown?*

— *E. E. Hewitt*

# CHAPTER 6
# Stars in my Crown

On Sundays all the stores closed, and we spent mornings and evenings in Asbury Methodist Church. One of many Methodist churches founded or aided by members of the Duke family, Asbury had come into being late in the nineteenth century when Benjamin Duke proposed the idea of establishing a church in West Durham, close to the new Erwin Cotton Mills, in order to minister to the spiritual needs of mill employees. Reuben Hibberd, a local florist and lay preacher, began conducting cottage prayer meetings and Bible classes in the homes of those villagers who favored the project; when enthusiasm began to grow and the worshippers became too numerous to fit into their hosts' small frame houses, the Sunday-School was moved to the grandstand of Trinity College's baseball park, only a block or two away from the mill neighborhood.[1] Subsequently, in the spring of 1894, Mr. Hibberd conducted revival services at the park; when the revival ended, forty-four persons — ten new converts, the rest transfers from other congregations — had indicated an interest in becoming members of the proposed

[1]The church's history, *The Asbury Trail*, points out that Mr. Hibberd was assisted by Alexander Smith, a devout man and a skilled cobbler who frequently handed his waiting customers a Bible to read, suggesting gently that they mend their souls while he repaired their shoes.

church. At the Annual Conference that same year the new congregation was assigned a pastor, the Reverend Robert W. Bailey, and in 1895 the congregation christened itself the West Durham Methodist Episcopal Church, South. About two years later Benjamin Duke donated to the young church a lot at the corner of West Main and Ninth Streets, where he then had a small chapel constructed; the Methodists shared that facility with the newly assembled West Durham Presbyterians until the latter could build their own church a few blocks away.

West Durham Methodist remained at its Main and Ninth Street location for nearly thirty years, until the church's growth finally occasioned a decision to move. During the mid-1920's the congregation purchased a lot on the corner of College and Sixth Streets (now Markham and Clarendon) and sold its Main Street property for $42,500. With the aid of a bank loan as well as another generous gift from Benjamin Duke, the Methodists constructed on the new site their present sanctuary — a simple, dignified, Romanesque building of dark red brick, with three arched doors across the front.

On Sunday, 14 August 1927, the new church formally opened its doors. The sanctuary was filled to overflowing, and extra chairs were brought in from the Sunday-School rooms; next day the *Herald* reported,

> Presbyterians, Baptists, and Episcopalians sat side by side with Methodists from various churches in the city, and entered into the service which launched the new edifice upon what is expected to be a long life of service to the community in pointing the way for countless hundreds to eternal life and mansions in the sky.

Pastor J. A. Martin expressed the congregation's joy in the new house of worship, and recognized a teacher in Raleigh's State School for the Blind for having made the first contribution to the cause: that person's one dollar gift had been placed in the hands of two church members, and had multiplied into over one hundred dollars in a few months' time. W. A. Erwin reminisced on the early religious life of West Durham, spoke of his interest in the church from its early days as a millworkers' prayer group, and expressed his delight at the realization of the members' long-cherished dream of a new edifice.

Duke University, only two years old in its new identity, played a major role in the opening service. Dr. Godbey of the School of Religion offered a prayer for divine guidance in the operation of the church, that it might successfully advance the purposes of God's kingdom on earth. President William P. Few delivered a sermon expressing his pride in being one of the church's neighbors; calling for those present to dedicate themselves to the service of God, he observed,

> Life is scarcely worth while unless you make up your mind to give the best in you to the world. Nobody who hasn't dedicated his life to something higher than self knows anything about the zest of human life....Life is a hard load to carry unless properly adjusted to it, but it is a beautiful thing for the spirit to give itself to the better and more enduring things of life.

The *Herald* reporter pointed out that because of its convenient proximity to Duke University, the church would attract many young men and women who were pursuing higher education in Durham: while the University offered instruction in science, history, and English, the church would provide knowledge of God and His teachings.

The new building, continued the reporter, was "one of the city's prettiest churches," a magnificent structure with its hard pine floors, stained glass windows, and six chandeliers. The edifice contained a large social hall along with several separate Sunday-School rooms (the classroom for mothers was located close to the Cradle Roll in order that mothers could have their classes within calling distance of their children). Of the construction cost of $88,000, a balance of $35,000 remained to be paid.

Thrift, fund-raising projects, and stubborn determination

enabled the church members, nearly all of whom were of moderate means, to squeeze out small annual mortgage payments throughout the Depression; in 1941 — aided, ironically, by the new prosperity arising from the nation's preparations for war — the congregation managed at last to retire its debt, and the church was formally dedicated. A few years later the membership voted to change the church's name from West Durham to Asbury Methodist, dropping the name that betokened the church's neighborhood origin in favor of one that honored the memory of America's first Methodist bishop and thus would presumably appeal to Methodists throughout the city. (The words "Episcopal" and "South" had already been dropped from the original name in 1939, when — nearly seventy-five years after the close of the Civil War — the Northern and Southern divisions of the church finally made their peace while simultaneously uniting with the Methodist Protestants.) At home, much to my parents' alarm, I took great umbrage at what seemed a cruel and deliberate effort to rob me of something familiar by changing my church's name: I wept inconsolably with the furious grief of a six-year-old, but the alteration took place anyway. And Asbury Methodist the church remains to this day, with the addition of "United" during the late 1960's to indicate another union, this time a unification of Methodists with the Evangelical United Brethren.

Most of the time, though, no major changes of name (or indeed of anything else) were being made or contemplated, and the church seemed to me immutable and everlasting. We went there twice each Sunday — for Sunday-School and church in the morning, and then for another church service in the evening. I liked the evening service better because it was more relaxed, the sermon was shorter, and we sat close to the front and used the Cokesbury Hymnal to sing hymns everyone loved, about the old, rugged cross and the roll being called up yonder, and, more briskly, "Will there be any stars, any stars in my crown, When at evening the sun goeth down?" Sometimes members of the congregation could request their favorites, and then if the minister called on me I always asked for "The Church in the Wildwood," which I thought meant the small Presbyterian church in the countryside close to my grandfather's farm. If we'd already sung that one, I chose "In the Garden," whose words about coming to the garden alone, while the dew was still on the roses, made me think of our own back yard, where my mother sometimes sent me out early in the morning to pick flowers for her circle meeting that evening. Sometimes we could persuade our minister's daughters to sing "Whispering Hope," and then we listened contentedly to their slow, sweet harmony, all the time fanning ourselves with wooden-handled cardboard fans, Compliments of Hall-Wynne Funeral Home.

To make up for the small size of the evening assembly everyone sang enthusiastically, filling the church almost as loudly with music as did the larger morning congregation, which tended to dress up more and sing such stately hymns as "Holy, Holy, Holy" and "Lead On, O King Eternal." In the mornings we always sat at the back, on the left-hand side of the church: my mother and I went in to sit down well before the service began and my father joined us just before the second anthem, after he'd walked proudly to the communion rail with the other ushers to present the offerings. When I was small I liked best to sit next to the end of the pew so I could lean my head up against the side when I got sleepy; but on the Sunday my father first served as an usher I enthusiastically stood up on the seat to wave to him each time he walked by, and from then on my mother made certain I sat on her other side, away from the aisle. To minimize my squirming restlessness during the sermon she always brought along a pencil and paper so I could entertain myself by drawing pictures; and early on, my artistic gifts

149

revealed themselves in such productions as a house with smoke curling aggressively out of its chimney, a duck that resembled a chicken, a rabbit with its tail in front. After I became a little older, though, my parents decided that drawing pictures during church was no longer acceptable: it was time for me to assume a more mature demeanor and begin paying attention to the service. Thereafter, when the sermon began I read the Methodist Hymnal for a while and then looked up to study the ten pairs of tall, arched, stained-glass windows that lined the sanctuary. After surveying each pair to identify the symbol in the tiny circle at the top — a cross, a white dove, a Bible — I focused carefully on a single window and began counting its individual pieces of stained glass. Generally I lost track at about a hundred and forty-five, and then I ran through whatever verses I could remember, beginning with "Columbus crossed the Delaware / In fourteen ninety-two." After that I mentally doubled numbers as far as I could go. By the time I stalled at four thousand ninety-six, usually the sermon had ended and it was time to stand for the closing hymn, the minister's blessing, the Sevenfold Amen, and the three chimes that heralded the close of the service. Those chimes were lovely, but tricky: they made it easy to spot visitors, who, as the Amens faded out, stepped confidently into the aisle to leave and then froze, disconcerted at realizing they had been the only ones to stir while the rest of the congregation waited motionless (though poised expectantly for departure) until the chimes ceased.

Several times a year we celebrated The Lord's Supper, and then the sermon was pleasingly short and we all got to walk solemnly down the carpeted aisles to kneel at the rail, drink grape juice out of tiny glasses, and swallow thin white wafers that looked exactly like the ones I bought at Kress's to feed my goldfish. When I checked with my Sunday-School teacher about it, though, she said no, these were special consecrated, unleavened bread just like what the Jews had used to celebrate

Passover. This seemed hard to believe, and I worried about it for several months; but finally I decided she was probably right, and anyway if the wafers didn't hurt the fish, they wouldn't hurt me.

My religious convictions were benevolent, but confused. It was clear, though, that if you went to church each Sunday and recited "Now I Lay Me Down To Sleep" every night (hurrying through "If I should die before I wake" so as not to give God any ideas), adding a postscript about being sorry for your sins, which it seemed you had plenty of to be sorry for even when you'd tried really hard to be good, then when you died you could look forward to going to heaven — a large open space just above the clouds — either immediately or else at some indefinite future time when Gabriel would blow his trumpet, and all the dead people in the world would rise simultaneously from their graves to be resurrected. In my mind's eye Heaven was quite crowded: everyone there wore a long white nightgown, and as far as I could tell they just milled around and mumbled a lot about things that didn't matter, much like the adults of my acquaintance. In the midst of the white-clad heavenly conversationalists stood God, also wearing a white robe: He was authoritative, balding, bespectacled, and slightly rotund, and He looked remarkably like Dr. Roberts, my pediatrician.


Sunday-School kept us nearly as busy as fourth grade. We made construction-paper scrapbooks neatly titled "Christmas" that contained painstakingly-lettered carol verses together with colored pictures cut from greeting cards and the *Woman's Home Companion;* sang "Tell Me The Stories of Jesus"; and planted shallow, pebble-filled green glass bowls with narcissus bulbs that sent up green shoots and then produced fragrant white blossoms, just in time for Easter Sunday. We memorized the

151

Twenty-Third and Hundredth Psalms, the Lord's Prayer and the Apostles' Creed, the Beatitudes and the Ten Commandments; and we learned to sing the names of the Old Testament books to the helpful tune of "Twinkle, Twinkle, Little Star." Ignoring all prohibitions against laying up treasures on earth, I busily amassed a collection of Sunday-School attendance pins, illustrated Bible story folders, ornate promotion certificates, and a post card explaining the religious symbolism of the dogwood.

Holidays were filled with excitement. On Easter, no matter how rainy or cold the weather, the women and girls blossomed out in new spring dresses, corsages, and flowered hats so that the church was transformed into a bower of pink, yellow, and green; on Mother's Day the women who had children were asked to stand and be recognized during the morning service, and we all wore red flowers in their honor. September brought Homecoming Sunday, when former members returned to join the congregation in a special service; afterward, on the Woman's College lawn just across the street, we had a splendid covered-dish luncheon that always included platters heaped high with fried chicken and ham; mounds of potato salad; bowls of cole slaw, green beans, and squash; and homemade desserts by the dozen — chocolate, pecan, and chess pies in the flakiest of crusts, and meltingly delicious devil's food and coconut cakes.

Asbury looked benevolently not only on the strictly Christian traditions but on those of less sacred origin as well. At Christmastime, wearing bathrobes and sheets, we tiptoed into the hushed, candlelit, red poinsettia-banked sanctuary to enact for the congregation solemn pageants about Joseph, Mary, and the Baby Jesus, while on Easter Sunday afternoon — much relieved that the agonizing suffering none of us liked to think about had ended, and He was safely Risen — we joyfully raced each other to find the colored eggs our teachers had cleverly hidden in and around the shrubbery on our church lawn. And one Hallowe'en the junior and senior high students worked for days to transform the old, church-owned frame residence next door into a haunted house: in the dimly-lit parlor rested a Clyde Kelly Funeral Home casket in which lay the normally vivacious Sandy Scott, wearing chalk-white makeup and a black dress. When callers entered the room she groaned, opened her eyes to gaze unseeingly ahead, and then rose slowly and majestically to a sitting position, eliciting satisfying gasps (and occasionally screams) from the impressionable in her audience.

Sunday mornings in the Primary Department meant Bible stories in either the language of King James or the simpler versions of Egermeier's; we liked them all, except for the account of God's testing of Abraham. The very first full-page colored picture in my Bible showed Isaac, dressed in white and with his hands and feet bound, lying on a pile of wood fagots atop a stone altar while Abraham, bearded and wearing a long blue robe, lifted his hands to the sky, presumably in worshipful obedience. In his right hand gleamed a wicked-looking knife, and beside the altar flamed a firebrand, ready to light the fire for the sacrifice. No matter how often our teachers explained about God's having to assure himself of Abraham's devotion, all of us disliked the story: our fathers would never treat *us* that way, we argued, and we thought it strange of God to require such a dreadful thing of His faithful servant Abraham, even if He was just testing.

Other stories were better. Clearly Noah was right to have obeyed God by building the Ark and saving all the animals so I could have my dog, cats, and goldfish, and Mr. Barnes next door could raise his goats. Joseph's coat of many colors excited our imaginations (each of us colored our own vivid version on construction paper), and we admired the faith that had enabled men to stroll triumphantly through a fiery furnace. And we all reveled in the surprise of Pharaoh's daughter on discovering the baby Moses in the bulrushes: at home I carefully covered my tiny blue plastic cradle with Scotch tape and floated it in our bathroom lavatory, noting with pleasure that my pink baby doll inside stayed safe and dry, just like Moses.

Partly because my mother was Superintendent of the Primary Department and therefore strategically placed to hear about any less-than-desirable behavior on my part, I worked hard at being one of the Sunday-School's star pupils; but my loving kindness was severely strained the day I took Jack Lester, my four-year-old neighbor, to visit our class of six-year-old Beginners. The occasion began well: uncustomarily wavy-haired (thanks to rag curlers the night before) and resplendent in my red velvet coatdress with matching bonnet and muff, I met Jack at our classroom door and introduced him to Mrs. Porter with what I considered gracious charm. Jack conducted himself reasonably well during the Bible stories and prayer, and only three times did I have to take him to the bathroom next door with its miniature, foot-high toilet. But he didn't know the words to "Jesus Wants Me For A Sunbeam" or "Praise Him, Praise Him"; and so every time we stood up to sing, Jack threw himself loudly and tunelessly into a chorus of his own favorite song:

> Lay that pistol down, babe,
> Lay that pistol down.
> Pistol-packin' mama,
> Lay that pistol down.

So loudly, in fact, that he tended to drown out the Beginners around him, who naturally became confused as to exactly which song was being sung, and one by one trailed off into puzzled silence. I myself gazed straight ahead, loftily disregarding the dissenter, but I longed to kill him. Tight-lipped and grim, I returned my guest to his mother after Sunday-School with scarcely a word of farewell, and for nearly a week afterward I refused even to invite him inside my house for Kool-Aid, let alone go over to sit in his umbrella tree. Eventually I softened: my mother's gentle murmurs about tolerance and understanding finally made an impression, and about the same time Jack called to say he was saving a package of chocolate marshmallow cookies for the next time I came over. We became friends again; but I stayed touchy about the Sunday-School incident for quite a while, and several months passed before it again seemed like a good idea to invite Jack Lester to visit my Beginners' class.

Church offered activities for us all. My mother belonged to an evening circle so my father would be home with me while she went out to meetings; the house became eerily quiet and empty when she left, but when she returned she always brought me a carefully wrapped paper napkin that when opened revealed two angel food squares topped with white icing, perhaps even a rose. Circle membership involved more than refreshments and conversation: during the years when the congregation was laboring to retire the church mortgage, the Women's Society served so many fundraising dinners that one longsuffering husband glumly observed, "This church building will never stand, because its foundation is made of brunswick stew."

Calmly overlooking such peccadillos as those of the boys who invaded the boiler room and nearly set the church on fire, Asbury loved its children and provided them with dedicated teachers as well as basketball teams, Scout troops, and hayrides. The junior choir was my favorite, though, and for six years I walked proudly with the rest in dignified white-robed procession on those special occasions when we sang anthems either alone or with the senior choristers. When I turned fourteen I joined the adult group, which enjoyed the reputation of being one of the best church choirs in the city. We had fine soloists in every range: first sopranos Cynthia Parrish and Ann Scarboro soared effortlessly to high G in "O For The Wings Of A Dove," while Gladys Bunting and Susan Butler contributed their rich alto warmth to "Fairest Lord Jesus." I, a perfectly ordinary second soprano, secretly harbored an unsaintly envy of them all. Thanks to Mrs. Twaddell's conscientious training I did read music, could carry a tune, and generally managed to make a joyful noise; fortunately for the sensitivities of the congregation, though, I was never required to sing even in a duet, let alone solo. In fact few of us had had formal voice training, but under Bill Ross's encouraging, gentle direction we stoutly tackled the harmonics of pieces from "How Lovely Is Thy Dwelling Place" to Handel's *Messiah*. And though we sometimes felt anxious, our performances almost always sounded splendid.

The choir sang two anthems each Sunday, the first early in the service and the second just before the sermon. As we sat down after the second piece, one of the baritones unobtrusively turned off the lights in the choir loft so that the congregation's attention shifted from us to the minister as he stood to deliver his sermon. Relaxing in the semi-shadows, I could entertain myself by discreetly observing the congregation to see which women were wearing new hats, whose children were misbehaving, and who had drifted peacefully off to sleep. One June morning when a nervous young pastor spoke his first words in Asbury, raising his already sonorous voice to the level he judged necessary to carry in a sanctuary much larger than that of his former church, several dozing members of the congregation jumped, looked around anxiously to see where the sound was coming from, and stayed awake for their first full sermon in years.

My father belonged to the Fred Thomas Bible Class, a large and enthusiastic men's group that each year planned, organized, and staffed the church's Christmas Tree Sale. Early in December fresh cedars and spruces of all sizes filled a vacant lot on Broad Street, just a block west of the church; and each man in the class took his turn working at the sale, occasionally huddling close to a fire for warmth during the long winter evenings. At the time artificial trees had found little popularity; and since that particular West Durham neighborhood had few stores offering Christmas trees, the sale always bustled with customers and netted a comfortable profit that eased the church's perennially tight budget. Of much more interest to the children in the congregation was the class's annual Christmas party in our fellowship hall: one of the men dressed as Santa Claus to hand out gifts, one for each child, from under a huge cedar tree that had been splendidly bedecked with dozens of colored lights, glass balls, icicles, and strings of popcorn. Dazzled by the glitter, I kept to the back of the room with my mother and father, waiting breathlessly to see whether Santa would call out my name and present me ceremoniously with a red or blue tissue-wrapped package — a new jump rope, perhaps, or a covered hobnail glass bowl filled with ribbon candy. And miraculously, he always did.

Most popular of all the Fred Thomas Class's fund-raising activities was their occasional Womanless Wedding, for which the burliest men in the class squeezed into bridesmaids' dresses, guests' afternoon attire, and a wedding gown and veil (invariably the bride towered over her groom by at least a foot). One of the smaller men, wearing makeshift baby clothes and holding a bottle, was transported into the wedding party in a carriage from which he petulantly flung out his rattle and disrupted the ceremony with angry wails that — loud as they were — didn't begin to match in volume the laments contributed by the mother of the bride. One by one the rouged, bewigged men teetered in on high heels to simper, mince, and clown their way through the ceremony, much of it *ad lib*: broad hilarity reigned, a capacity crowd filled Fellowship Hall, and everyone at Asbury looked forward for months to Womanless Weddings.

The church conducted its Vacation Bible School each June, every morning for two weeks; and one year's session had barely ended when I began looking forward to the next. We spent quite a lot of time studying Palestine and enjoying snacks of grape juice, fig newtons, and Golden Fruit Raisin Biscuits; sometimes, though, we strung macaroni necklaces, wove baskets, or made pinked-edge bookmarks carefully lettered God Is Love, and each day we crossed the street to the grassy expanse of Duke's East Campus, to play Farmer in the Dell and London Bridge. At the end of the two-week session teachers, students, and parents attended an impressive closing exercise in the sanctuary at which the minister spoke and we were awarded certificates decorated with full-color pictures of Jesus preaching the Sermon on the Mount; afterwards our parents had a chance to inspect our displays of bookmarks, baskets, and Scrapbooks On Helping Others.

Bible School was so much fun that for a couple of years I attended not only Asbury's but also one at a Baptist church close to our house. As I completed my second year there, we gathered as usual on Friday evening for the closing exercise; about two-thirds of the way through, when we had already marched to the front of the church, received our certificates, and returned to our pews, the pastor began without warning to talk about baptism. Something he said gave me the idea that all of us who'd attended Bible School were to be baptized — actually immersed in the pool that was ominously visible at the front of the church — *right then.* Since I was struggling hard that summer to overcome my fear of going underwater, the prospect of being forcibly immersed filled me with instant terror. To make matters worse I was sitting not with my parents, who would have protected me, but with my classmates, where I would have to do whatever the others did, or else be conspicuous by my refusal. As the seconds dragged on, the knot in my stomach became colder; when at last I could bear the fear no longer I anxiously nudged my teacher to ask was it true, were we really to be baptized that evening? Perceiving my anguish, she assured me that we weren't, and I was partially comforted; but only when the service ended and I could leave the church to return to the more secure sanctuary of my parents' safekeeping, did I relax. The next summer the Baptist church counted one less Bible Scholar. My nervous conclusion, admittedly ill-founded, had been that Baptists were unpredictable, perhaps even dangerous, in their zeal to immerse. Best to keep a safe distance, just in case.

My uneasiness notwithstanding, some of our best friends were Baptists. Because the Dukes had been exceptionally supportive Methodists,[2] Durham itself always seemed preeminently Methodist; but in fact, as in every Southern town, the Baptists and the Presbyterians counted sizeable numbers of their faithful as well. Nearly everyone we knew belonged to one of those three comfortable, familiar denominations; beyond them existed, in my mind at least, an oddly assorted collection of churches, assemblies, and sects whose differences I failed even to perceive, let alone understand. Jumbled together in this heterogeneous company were such groups as the Jehovah's Witnesses and Primitive Baptists, the Church of God, and the Gospel Center with its weekly radio broadcasts (Message by Welcome Detweiler). Occasionally other groups appeared: Oral Roberts sometimes came to conduct a week of tent services, Healing Line Each Night, down in East Durham; his converts were said to number in the hundreds, but no one I knew ever went. And for years one of Durham's best-known sights was a short, heavy-set, white-robed and headdressed black woman who strode briskly throughout town declaiming "The Spirit of the *Lord*! Told *Me*! To Tell the *World*! That *Je*-sus! Is Soon to *COME*!" It was said that the woman was a

[2]One of Benjamin Duke's most urgent concerns had been the welfare of "worn out" Methodist clergymen; Brodie Duke had donated land for the Main Street Methodist Church. The Dukes had provided financial support to Methodist Trinity College for years before James B. Duke's Endowment effected its transformation into Duke University.

Heavenly Light, a disciple of Father Divine; whether that was true or she was prophesying from her own powerful inner vision, I never knew.

Located on the more exotic fringes of this mysterious collection was the Zion Tabernacle, whose members believed that handling poisonous snakes during church services proved one's faith and indicated that he or she was safely sheltered under Divine Protection.[3] (It was also a dead-certain way of drawing a crowd.) One of two things always happened to bring the chanting, moaning services to a temporary stop: the snakes became wakeful and active in the warm building at the same time that there occurred a slippage of Divine Protection, causing an inattentive handler to be bitten; or else police invaded the services, halting the shrieking, orgiastic frenzy to arrest the sect's leaders and confiscate the large rattlers and copperheads. Next day the *Herald* reported matter-of-factly on whatever had happened, sometimes with an accompanying photograph revealing the sect's leader, his expression ecstatic, wearing a large rattlesnake draped around his neck or on his head, while the men and women of the assembly prayed or shouted, their eyes glassy and uplifted and their faces as rapturous as their leader's. After the denouement, quiet reigned temporarily in the Tabernacle. Belief persisted despite all obstacles, though, and only a few months would pass before the enthusiasts provided themselves with a new collection of snakes, to try again.

At the other end of the religious spectrum, though no less foreign to most of us than were the shouters and the snakehandlers, were the Episcopalians and the Catholics, who exuded an indefinable air of belonging, security, and — somehow —

---

[3]"And these signs shall follow them that believe; In my name shall they cast out devils; they shall speak with new tongues;

"They shall take up serpents; and if they drink any deadly thing, it shall not hurt them...."

Mark 16: 17,18

an inside track to Divinity. We knew, of course, that Catholics did whatever the Pope ordered, but in practical terms the differences between the two groups seemed slight. It appeared that both Episcopalians and Catholics knelt during their worship services, a practice that to our literal Methodist minds seemed almost unbearably exotic; it was rumored, too, that members of both churches openly Drank Alcohol. For their Lord's Supper, which they referred to oddly as Holy Communion or Mass, we heard they used real wine in a big silver cup that everyone sipped from, rather than grape juice in tiny, aseptic glasses.

A few years later, when we spent several Sunday evenings Understanding Other Religions in Senior MYF meetings, it developed that Understanding Catholicism was even tougher than we'd thought. All of us girls had been impressed by a recent *Photoplay* picture that showed the lovely, pure, and very Catholic Ann Blyth gazing solemnly at the gold wedding band she was soon to receive from her obstetrician fiancé; but then when we started getting into specifics, it appeared that — far from just wearing becoming little prayer veils and basking in holiness all the time — the faithful also had to sit through endless and incomprehensible services in Latin, as well as run the risk of going to hell for eating meat on Friday, or for missing Sunday church. It appeared, too, that the worst mistake a Protestant girl could make would be to fall in love with a Catholic boy, because in order to marry him she would have to convert to his religion, thus turning her back forever on her family (who, simultaneously furious and heartbroken, would disown her and never again allow her name to cross their lips), as well as swear to bring up all her children as Catholics (and the children would number at least eight or ten, and if the wife had any trouble in childbirth her husband would callously instruct the doctor to save the baby and let his wife die). Walking out of Fellowship Hall afterwards, we all thought the evening's report interesting; it seemed, though, to offer slim hope of Understanding

Catholicism since on reflection most of us had concluded that we were better off in a church that refrained from meddling too much in its members' private lives. And anyway, as Doris Rhew sensibly pointed out, how could a Methodist ever find much in common with a group of people who hoped someday to go to Rome and kiss the Pope's toe?

*Praise the Lord and Pass the Ammunition.*

— *Title of song*
*by Frank Loesser*

# CHAPTER 7
# Praise the Lord
# And Pass The Ammunition

**W**ithin three months after the Japanese had attacked Pearl Harbor, the country had undergone a radical change: "conserve," "patch," "make it last," "do without," became the catchwords of the day. That Spartan stance would endure for four years while nearly every company, every service turned its energies toward war. One after another, manufacturers explained that at present their factories and raw materials were being used to produce war supplies, but that when the conflict ended, new automobiles, sheets, appliances, nylon stockings would appear in abundance. (Midway in the war it was reported that although civilians were amiably doing without refrigerators and washers, they complained about shortages of pots and pans, elastic tape, and bobby pins.) Point rationing quickly appeared on food, gasoline, and shoes. Greyhound apologized for its inadequacies while it was "short on buses and long on passengers — doin' our best to serve the Armed Forces" and pledged better service in the future, "as sure as Nippon's 'rising sun' will set."

Citing heavy demand on depleted ranks of medical personnel, Spare The Doctor ads urged civilians to guard their good health in order to call on physicians as infrequently as possible. Telephone companies enjoined subscribers to answer the

165

telephone promptly, make calls brief, and keep voices calm and controlled. Fighters on the home front received constant reminders about insulating their houses (thereby conserving fuel), eliminating unnecessary travel, and turning in anything that could be transformed into armaments — fats, rubber, nylon stockings, scrap metal of all kinds. (A *New Yorker* cartoon pictured an eager Boy Scout troop, laden with metal salvage, standing expectantly on the front steps of a house from which two negligeed young women peer curiously out of the window; at the door stands a slightly harried but voluptuous middle-aged woman, dressed in a décolleté peignoir and impatiently informing the young patriots, "I tell you we haven't *got* any aluminum!")

The war touched everything. A stern Uncle Sam pointed his finger straight at passersby from posters on nearly every building, declaring roundly that he wanted YOU for the U.S. Army. Stores gave defense stamps as dividends with purchases; used car dealers earnestly assured the public that their merchandise boasted Tires With Plenty Of Rubber. Coca-Cola

---

*Things you can do to save every ounce of rubber left in your tires*

1. Never drive unless it is absolutely necessary.
2. Never drive alone . . . Share your car.
3. Have your tires recapped *in time* to save them.
4. Have your tires inflated every week or two.
5. Baby your tires . . . Start and stop slowly; slow down on curves.
6. Avoid curbs, ruts, especially pavement-breaks, now more serious because of wartime necessity.

---

*Advertisement for U.S. Rubber, 1943.*

ads pictured clean-cut American servicemen happily discovering that "Have a Coke" was understood throughout the world. Lucky Strike green went to war, and never came back. Science museums along the East and West Coast shipped thousands of specimens, from insects to great auks, to bank vaults and bomb shelters for safety. The Wisconsin Liars' Club announced that it would prepare for its annual meeting by listening to Axis broadcasts in Europe. U.S. liquor companies converted their output to war alcohol, four gallons of which were required to produce a single synthetic tire. At home, my playmates and I sang the Marine Hymn alternately with "Mairzy Doats," and busily scribbled "Kilroy was here" everywhere we went.

Drugstore card racks held special greetings for servicemen (usually such cards had pictures of tanks, battleships, or fighter planes; and the sentiments inside tended to be generalized, occasionally obscure). Windows in homes revealed families' contributions to the war effort: a star on a satin flag betokened a son or brother in service; when the star was changed to gold, one knew the contribution had become sadly final. Even cartoon characters did their bit — Joe Palooka joined the Army, and Smilin' Jack the Army Air Corps, while Daddy Warbucks served as a general. (Superman, though, was classified 4-F. When he took an eye test during his pre-induction physical, his X-ray vision looked straight through the chart and then the wall behind it, to read a different chart in the next room. Though disappointed, he accepted the rejection manfully, and spent the war years selling War Bonds and publicizing the Red Cross.)

An army marches on its stomach, advised Napoleon; and across the land farmers and food suppliers turned much of their effort into feeding the country's fighting men. Back home, soldiers without guns were urged to supply as many as possible of their own food needs by cultivating gardens; and soon pamphlets and newspaper articles flooded the fledgling farmers with information on how to can their presumably bountiful harvest. Magazines offered advice on utilizing leftovers — on feeding one's family well while staying within meat and cheese allowances — on baking without butter, or without sugar, or without eggs. (The butterless, sugarless, eggless cake attacked on all three fronts at once.) Sage, saffron, and thyme vanished early in the war. At the White House, desserts virtually disappeared from the table while leftovers made encore appearances gracefully disguised as stew, ragout, and hash; those remainders considered beyond hope went to nourish pigs at a nearby cooperative farm. Twentieth-Century-Fox sympathetically announced that it would cut large banquet scenes from its films. And a few miles outside Durham, in Rougemont, an eleven-year-old boy aided the war effort by selling his most prized possession — his bicycle — in order to buy a cow that would provide milk for himself and his family. (*Herald* readers, touched by the newspaper's account of the boy's sacrifice, contributed enough money to buy him a new bicycle.)

The famous met the demands of war in differing ways. In Great Britain, King George VI cut fuel and electricity use in Buckingham Palace and Windsor Castle by limiting all tub baths to five inches of water (warning lines were painted at the five inch level), issuing only one light bulb for each bedroom, and prohibiting use of bedroom fireplaces except on doctors' orders. Tallulah Bankhead gallantly offered her blood, at the same time warning that as she was so anemic that her blood would doubtless kill any good American soldier, it should be put into Japanese soldiers instead. The beautiful comedienne Carole Lombard, returning home from a whirlwind national tour during which she had sold millions of dollars worth of War Bonds, died when her plane crashed in the mountains of Nevada. Judy Garland's recording of "The Last Time I Saw Paris" poignantly expressed the sadness of millions of Americans who — though most of them, like Miss Garland, had never visited France — felt that when the City of Light was darkened, the entire western world had suffered from the loss. Bing Crosby's rendition of Irving Berlin's "White Christmas" quickly took its own place in the mystique of the war: for U.S. servicemen who faced lonely, tropical holidays from North Africa to the South Pacific, the song touched a chord of instant response. Sonja Henie applied to Lloyd's for insurance ($250,000) on her last five pairs of ice skates, which because of wartime metal restrictions could not be replaced. Actor Jimmy Stewart received the Distinguished Flying Cross for his service as a squadron commander in the Eighth Air Force; and Bob Hope, traveling indefatigably to entertain the troops in nearly every U.S. camp, soon became a legend in his time.

As news turned bleak and the war dragged on, many turned to religion. Bible sales increased; novels with spiritual themes made the bestseller lists; Mary Tileston's *Daily Strength for Daily Needs* doubled its peacetime sales. Church attendance likewise increased, and membership reached an all-time high. Pacifism was nearly non-existent; but one conscientious objector received the Congressional Medal of Honor for his courage and dedication as an Army Medical Corpsman: while serving on Okinawa, he had rescued dozens of wounded men in the face of constant enemy fire. Much more prevalent than pacifism was the view of Swiss Calvinist Karl Barth who, having reversed his pre-war stand that battle never solved anything, declared the conflict in Europe to be "a righteous war, which God commands us to wage ardently." In total accord with Barth's philosophy were the reactions of a Pearl Harbor battleship chaplain who had just begun preparing for divine service when the Japanese attacked. The chaplain raced to an anti-aircraft gun, opened fire, and in a few seconds was heard to shout, "Praise the Lord and pass the ammunition — I just got one of the sons of bitches!"

No sooner had the war effort called, than U.S. women by the thousands answered: as industry converted its output to airplanes, guns, and tanks, women moved in to work on the assembly lines. Nine months after Pearl Harbor, *Time* amused itself by enumerating problems arising from the new employees' presence (the women were flirtatious and distractingly sexy, and they created safety hazards by refusing to cover their hair).

Despite such difficulties, the magazine conceded, when the women were good, they were very, very good: they were painstaking inspectors, quick and nimble with their fingers, good at assembling small parts — and they didn't fret or get bored with repetitious work. Occasionally women workers adopted their own methods of maximizing defense production: in Portland, female employees of the Albina Engine and Machine Works signed "No Work, No Woo" pledges in which they promised not to date any Albina man who had less than perfect job attendance for the week.

When women's branches of the services were created, more thousands hastened to sign up as WAACs, WAVEs, and WAFs; after enduring the inevitable raillery that followed, they proceeded to serve honorably in dozens of non-combat situations, as drivers, clerks, mechanics, and pilots. Women who remained at home to rear families had perhaps the most demanding, least-praised jobs of all — juggling limited ration allowances and budgets to feed and clothe growing children, coping with frequent shortages, maintaining the morale of loved ones at home as well as in the service, and somehow — as many did — finding time to volunteer as a nurse's aide, or for the Red Cross. Despite millions of women's successful war service, though, when it came to maintaining servicemen's morale, one movie star's contribution may have matched anyone's: the famous rear view pinup of Betty Grable — wearing a snugly-fitted one-piece bathing suit, and smiling coyly over her shoulder straight into the onlooker's eyes — was considered an essential furnishing in barracks throughout the world.

Fashion likewise mobilized. The slacks and snoods that were *de rigueur* for Rosie the Riveter quickly became popular attire for women throughout the country, and Winston Churchill's comfortable air-raid suits were soon adapted for assembly line and leisure wear. Clothes took on a decided military air: the functional Eisenhower jacket became a drawstring-bottom crepe blouse, while evening gowns sported hip-to-shoulder decorations of sequined eagles' wings. Wartime regulations set strict limits on the amount of fabric that could be used to manufacture civilian garments — hems no more than two inches, only one patch pocket per blouse, no full skirts, no cuffs on coats, no attached hoods or shawls, no wide belts. Most women's (and *Vogue's*) favored daytime dress was a suit — a padded-shoulder jacket with short, pencil-slim skirt — worn over a simple, short-sleeved blouse (one pocket only, and *no* ruffles). But when the war ended and restrictions were finally lifted, the change came almost overnight: long-repressed couturiers let their fancies soar, and fashion exploded into a joyous frenzy of ruffles, flowers, and long, full skirts. The New Look had arrived.

\* \* \* \* \*

Wartime changes came early to Durham, for a site only ten miles outside the city was selected for construction of a wartime military installation, to be named Camp Butner. Hard on the heels of the initial announcement arrived a housing shortage: those who came to build the camp needed living accommodations, and Durhamites heard for the first time the plea that for the next five years would form a constant refrain — Rent Out Your Extra Bedrooms. Within a few months after the Pearl Harbor attack, Durham had become a sea of khaki, with a steady stream of military personnel traveling between Camp Butner and the city. (The Raleigh-Durham airport was taken over by the Army for pilot training.) The acceleration of activity had begun in mid-December, though, with the announcement that the 1942 Rose Bowl would be held at Duke: government officials feared that a large gathering on the West Coast might encourage the Japanese to launch a military strike. (According to a professor of that time, the change of location was unpopular with the Duke team and especially with the band, both of which had looked forward eagerly to the Pasadena trip. Students *en masse* suddenly felt sentimentally impelled to spend the holidays with their families instead of returning to school in time to attend the game; and, noted the professor disapprovingly, "What should have been a great occasion degenerated into a drab affair.")

With Camp Butner so close, the war took on a special, intimate urgency. Van Straaten's and Pritchard-Bright carried complete stocks of officers' uniforms, gabardine trench coats, accessories and insignia. Durham Transportation Corporation instituted a special bus service between Durham and Camp Butner, fifty-five cents per round trip. Local service clubs decorated the USO centers for Christmas, and young Durham women acted as hostesses in the social clubs at Camp Butner. Soldiers who dined in local restaurants frequently found their checks paid by hospitable Durhamites, who took special pride in "their" men in uniform; on holidays, dances and special programs for servicemen took place throughout the city. The Malbourne Hotel filled up early on weekends, and sometimes as many as fifty soldiers slept in the lobby — in chairs, on sofas, and on the floor. (Manager E. I. Bugg never charged those "overflow" guests, but allowed them every courtesy, including baths in the public rooms.)

Durham Public Service apologized frequently for its crowded buses, citing rationing of tires, gasoline, and metal as well as the added traffic to and from Camp Butner; in order to fill some of the draft-caused vacancies in its ranks, the company hired several women as bus drivers for the duration of the war. One of them quickly acquired the reputation of being an iron-fisted tyrant: few people were brash enough to argue with her, but once, when she ordered a male passenger to discard his cigar, the man politely objected, "I'm not smoking." Visibly annoyed, the driver pointed out, "You have a cigar in your mouth," whereupon the man retorted blandly, "I have shoes on my feet, but I'm not walking."

Central to everyone's consciousness was the newspaper. Together with carrying daily accounts of battlefield action in each theater of operations, the *Herald* issued orders for the battle on the home front as well as dispatches on its progress. Over and over local firms bought ads to recite the wartime litany: conserve gasoline and rubber, conserve food and electricity, save scrap metal and newspapers, rent out spare bedrooms, volunteer as a Nurse's Aide, go to church and pray for a victorious peace, and above all Buy War Bonds. Ads, along with

> ℞ "TAKE one or two War Bonds
> in regular doses,
> Keep calm and avoid
> an unhealthy 'psychosis,'
> Get plenty of exercise —
> salvaging steel;
> Be sure what you eat
> is a *nutritive* meal;
> Stay cheerful — yes, even
> when paying your taxes,
> And work with your neighbor
> to help smash the Axis!"

*Advertisement for Pabst Blue Ribbon, 1943.*

the Weekly War Ration Guide, tried valiantly to explain the intricacies of the point rationing system, which no one ever understood. Concern about careless talk prompted a combined radio and newspaper campaign advising, "If you hear it on the radio or read it in the paper, you can repeat it. If you hear it rumored, keep it to yourself"; urging citizens to "float a flag instead of a rumor," the *Sun* offered a 3'x5' flag set for $1.50. Offering special subscription rates to men and women in service, the *Herald* also published a "Week's News from Home" column, designed to be clipped and mailed to servicemen who were stationed overseas.

The columnists offered timely advice: Dorothy Dix advised on how to treat a returning veteran (with patience and forbearance, but with alertness to any failure to readjust to civilian life within a short time). Angelo Patri counselled on allaying children's wartime fears, and Genevieve Smith wrote on wartime buying and making one's dollar stretch. Perhaps more widely read than any other part of the newspaper were the columns of the beloved Ernie Pyle: writing an account of his walk on a Normandy beach the day after D-Day, Pyle began almost nonchalantly, "It was a lovely day for strolling along the seashore. Men were sleeping on the sand, some were sleeping forever" and continued with a moving account of the personal gear — Bibles, sewing kits, diaries, even a tennis racket — that lay jumbled in a row along the water's edge. (On June 7, Baldwin's sponsored a heart-stopping, quarter-page *Herald* ad that joyfully headlined the news: "Lafayette, we are here...again.")

Though several of my uncles served in the Armed Forces, our immediate family was fortunate enough to stay together throughout the war. My father, who was thirty-five when Pearl Harbor was attacked, would surely have been drafted had not his company requested his exemption, pointing out that his job was essential to the war effort. At home he became a block captain and was issued a weighty club that he kept in the top drawer of his chest, presumably to intimidate any reckless civilian who might disobey orders in an emergency. Once a month we had practice air raids and blackout drills, and then we turned out every light in the house to sit silent and apprehensive in my parents' darkened bedroom, gazing into the blackness outside, until the signal sounded, and the lights came back on, and we were safe once more.

Posters, newspapers, and magazines exhorted us to save, conserve, and economize; and we did. We collected used cooking fats, bundled newspapers, and saved every bit of scrap metal we could find — tin cans, empty toothpowder tins, squeezed-out toothpaste tubes. We carefully supplied the Scott and Roberts man with a hanger for each garment when he came to pick up our clothes for dry cleaning; and my mother took her own grocery bags to the Piggly Wiggly after the store announced that paper bags had gone to war. My father recapped the tires on our grey Plymouth, and the vegetable garden he grew each summer became a Victory Garden for the duration of the war. And we bought War Bonds: my father squeezed enough money from each paycheck to buy a $25 bond, and every few days I pasted defense stamps into a book until it was filled, and I could proudly turn it in for a bond of my own.

We had ration books for meat, butter and cheese, coffee, gasoline, shoes; rationing and shortages were so common, in fact, that when the war ended I was amazed to discover that the bananas I longed for were suddenly plentiful, and we no longer needed our coupon books to go shopping. During the rationing years one had to stay alert to coupon values, which altered whimsically from one week to the next; but my mother and the other soldiers in housedresses always read the *Herald*'s War Ration Guide, which each week provided the new equivalents for its readers' illumination.[1] Some people quietly patronized the black markets; but because our family was small, and my mother was imaginative about making clothes last and foods stretch — occasionally she augmented a meager meal with a side dish of fried squash blossoms — we had everything we needed without them. (Considering such measures unpatriotic in the extreme, my parents would almost certainly never have resorted to them anyway.)

[1]For example: "All RED and BLUE stamps in War Ration Book 4 are WORTH 10 POINTS EACH. RED and BLUE TOKENS are WORTH 1 POINT EACH. RED and BLUE TOKENS are used to make CHANGE for RED and BLUE stamps only when purchase is made. IMPORTANT! POINT VALUES OF BROWN and GREEN STAMPS are NOT changed."

We had roomers throughout the war. My mother had begun renting out a room or two early on, when construction began at Camp Butner; later on came servicemen and their wives and parents, so that for several years we had a steady stream of arrivals and departures. The need for housing was so acute that my mother never had to run a newspaper ad to rent out her rooms; more, she never dared to. Usually the procedure remained the same: when a soldier received orders to ship out, he mentioned quietly to a friend that a room would soon be available; the following week the friend's wife would move in, delighted at having the opportunity of spending a few weeks close to her husband. My parents could almost always find ways to "make do," and when necessary, our three bedrooms could become four: my father would move a bed into the sun parlor, and whoever stayed there simply closed the curtained French doors that opened into the living room. To further ease crowding, I slept in a small bed in my parents' room until the war ended, at which time the housing shortage eased and I was coincidentally deemed old enough to move into a room of my own. With all three of us in a single room, the house seemed more spacious than it really was; and frequently our small dwelling with its single bath housed, in addition to my parents and myself, three soldiers and their wives. And once in a while all three bedrooms unexpectedly emptied within a few hours, as orders arrived and a company shipped out.

For me, the only child in a houseful of adults energized by the ever-present awareness of war, life was filled with interest and excitement. The homesick soldiers and their wives petted and played with me: the young women painted my fingernails, provided an attentive audience as I rode my scooter, entertained me with "Itsy Bitsy Spider" and Old Maid, and let me watch as they coped with the shortage in stockings by skillfully applying liquid leg makeup, on top of which they drew seams with eyebrow pencil. The men carried me around on their shoulders, showed me their ribbons and medals, blew perfect smoke rings, and taught me to sing "Off we go, into the wild blue yonder," coming down hard at the end: "Nothing can stop the ARMY AIR CORPS!" In return I adored them, thinking them members of a sort of extended family, and weeping heartbrokenly when each one left. Several of them happy young newlyweds, most of our servicemen and their wives dropped out of contact within a few years; a few, though, stayed on in Durham after the war ended, and became our friends for life.

Occasional difficulties arose. Sometimes our roomers were frightened awake by early morning gunfire, which proved to be our next-door neighbor opening exasperated aim on the blue jays that brazenly plundered his huge pecan tree. One midnight my colored tin chicken, up till then my favorite toy, unexpectedly came alive and took on monstrous proportions to chase me down endless halls, whereupon my screams alarmed my parents and our guests alike into a state of jangled wakefulness that lasted until the next morning. One young bride usually had a heavy coating of dust in her room, the result of overgenerous use of talcum powder as a dry shampoo. From time to time linguistic perplexities appeared: our Northern guests habitually looked confused, even uneasy, on hearing that it was fixin' to rain dreckly, or that an aunt had fallen off a lot, or that someone was on the po'ly list, or that a neighbor had given my mother a mess of beans. (They were even more baffled when cut onions appeared on windowsills throughout the house, my mother's insurance against a cold's spreading between members of the household.) Nearly all the soldiers who stayed with us were gentlemanly and quiet; but once in a while, perhaps distressed by news from Europe, one would utter a mild oath, thereby causing my mother to glance meaningfully at my father, who would shortly find an opportunity to take the errant young man into another room for a brief talk. (Swearing was taboo at our house. I was allowed

to give vent to strong emotion with "heck" and "doggone it,"
but my freedom ended with attempts at expanding my
vocabulary to include "darn" and "dern," which my parents
thought unsuitable for a young girl. My father sometimes
indulged himself in an emphatic "Well, I *swanny!*" when he
was surprised or disturbed. I heard "damn" and "hell" only
in their literal senses and only in church, when a visiting
evangelist felt compelled to use strong language in order to
indicate the fate of the unsaved.)

Not all of our roomers were service-connected: midway in
the war an attractive elderly lady, a New Englander, became
a regular winter guest whose return I eagerly anticipated for
weeks each autumn. She sewed clothes for me, and played the
Nutcracker Suite on her phonograph so that I, for a few fleeting
moments an accomplished ballerina, could whirl dreamily and
blissfully down the hall; and on my fifth birthday she gave me
a charming miniature sink, equipped with a shallow tray in
back that when filled with water enabled the tiny faucet to
dispense a miniscule stream. (I was enchanted by the gift,
although — a war-wise, thrift-conscious child — I did somewhat
dampen the occasion by inquiring politely how much it had
cost.) And once she gave us a glorious week at her beach cottage
at Nags Head, where I splashed rapturously in white foam, and
scrutinized strange leggy creatures on the sand, and once
wandered, lost and tearful, between the houses — all on stilts,
and all ominously alike — until my father rescued me and took
me home.


When peace came, it came by degrees. Paris was liberated,
and a crowd in Rockefeller Plaza celebrated with confetti, ticker
tape, and cheering applause for Lily Pons, who — wearing her
USO uniform — triumphantly sang the Marseillaise; radio
announcers throughout the country played French songs all day

long. (It was barely a month later that the new fashions began to appear.) Early the following April the city's lights went back on, once more outlining the Champs Elysées and illuminating the Arc de Triomphe. May brought Victory in Europe; June saw an enthusiastic welcome home to General Eisenhower, together with an end to the nationwide cigarette shortage. Japan surrendered in August, and in the midst of the ecstatic crowd in Times Square a sailor bent a girl backward in an enthusiastic kiss, the photograph of which became one of the most reprinted images of the war. By September, life had begun a fairly rapid return to normal as the War Production Board allowed U.S. manufacturers to resume production of automobiles, washers, electric razors, and radios. (The Armed Services, meanwhile, were pondering how to dispose of excess war supplies that included a supply of Elizabeth Arden face cream, black; forty thousand homing pigeons; and ten million pounds of contraceptive jelly.) On the New Year's Eve that followed, the bars of Manhattan stayed open till dawn.

\* \* \* \* \*

One of the war's last unconfirmed tales emerged from Potsdam: despite the vigilance of those who had been assigned to guard the premises, rumor had it that a confused-looking Josef Stalin had emerged from a portable toilet to inquire confidentially of an aide, "Who was Kilroy?"

*"When you're alone,*
*and life is making you lonely,*
*You can always go — Downtown."*

— Tony Hatch

# CHAPTER 8
# Downtown

From the time I was eight or nine and therefore old enough to be downtown alone, Saturdays were pure bliss. Once in a while, especially when it rained, I stayed home long enough to join "Let's Pretend" at eleven, traveling with Uncle Bill Adams and the Cream of Wheat gang on a flock of geese or a stratocruiser to hear about exquisite princesses and enchanted frogs; usually, though, Saturdays began promptly at nine, when my mother deposited me at the door of the Durham Public Library.

The Library had had its beginnings at an 1896 meeting of the Canterbury Club, a literary and civic group that had as one of its aims the cultural improvement of the city. Trinity College's Professor Edwin Mims suggested to the Club's members that they begin a library movement, and the idea was accepted. After several leading citizens had promised their assistance, a citywide meeting took place during which citizens subscribed $4,000 to the project; Miss Lallah Ruth Carr, daughter of Julian S. Carr and a member of the Canterbury Club, donated to the cause a lot at the intersection of Main and Chapel Hill Streets. Since the building was expected to cost more than was raised at the organizational meeting, several of the town's prominent women organized a Board of Lady Governors of the Durham Public

Library, whose purpose was to raise additional funds and to oversee the project; this group raised an additional $1,700 in pledges, enabling construction of the building to take place during the following year.

On 10 February 1898 the Library opened its doors. The *Durham Daily Sun* of that date included a happy reminder to the townspeople:

> The day has arrived. The event takes place this evening. The Public Library will be opened....A good start with books. Now let us carry it on to a complete success.

The following day the *Sun* reported with pride on the new facility:

> The building is a beauty in its arrangements for comfort, convenience and service. One of the best to be found in the South, and it is estimated it now has some fifteen or sixteen hundred books of inestimable value, now on the shelves in its alcoves.

The frame Queen Anne building included eight alcoves for books as well as two rooms for reception, reading, and literary purposes (one room for ladies, the other for gentlemen).

On opening evening the rooms, decorated with numerous arrangements of fresh flowers, were crowded by six or seven hundred enthusiastic citizens who had come to witness the inauguration of the new facility. A special children's reception was held from 5 to 6 p.m., after which the library was opened to the people of Durham. The Reverend W. C. Tyree offered the invocation, asking God's blessings upon the institution and on the efforts that had produced it; James Southgate offered words of hope, encouragement, and congratulation, and announced on behalf of the committee that the library was now open and dedicated to the people of Durham as their property, and their pride. Major W. A. Guthrie responded on behalf of the town, commending those who had worked so diligently for the project's success. The Choral Society and the Durham

Orchestra offered musical selections, and at the program's conclusion the entire crowd sang "The Old North State" and "Dixie" with, as the *Sun* noted approvingly, "a gusto seldom heard in Durham." The forward-thinking philosophy of the new institution caused much comment: this library was the first in North Carolina to receive municipal support, as well as the first free public library in the state.

By 1911 the Library had acquired some 3500 volumes, somewhat unsystematically arranged by the volunteers who worked in the facility. At that point the City took the significant action of hiring a professional librarian, Lillian Baker Griggs. The first trained public librarian in the state, Mrs. Griggs was an energetic and enthusiastic woman who successfully expanded library services throughout the city and outside it as well: she opened branches in West Durham, East Durham, and Edgemont as well as starting libraries at Watts Hospital and Durham High School. She also initiated a bookmobile service, the first in North Carolina, and supervised the organization of a public library for blacks (this facility would later be named the Stanford L. Warren Public Library). On leaving the Durham Public Library in January of 1924 to become Director of the North Carolina Library Commission, Mrs. Griggs was succeeded by Miss Clara Crawford, who would hold the position for thirty-five years.[1]

Within a very few years of her arrival, Mrs. Griggs had pointed out to the Board of Trustees that the existing facility was inadequate for the Library's many activities. Despite the vehement opposition of Julian S. Carr, then Chairman of the Board, Mrs. Griggs and other trustees decided to approach the

[1]During its meeting of 6 November 1923, the Library's Board of Trustees adopted a resolution of appreciation for Mrs. Griggs's efforts that read in part, "...our regret at her resignation is inexpressibly great, and our loss seems irreparable. The community's debt to her will last as long as the Library continues its beneficent work."

Carnegie Corporation for funds to construct a new building; in the fall of 1917, the request was approved. A two years' delay ensued, occasioned primarily by Mrs. Griggs's war service; but in 1920, construction finally began. After the sale of the existing library property, Mrs. Griggs moved books and furnishings into temporary quarters at the Lochmoor Hotel, only a few hundred feet away from the new site on East Main Street, until construction could be completed.

The new library opened on the afternoon of 6 July 1921. A *Durham Morning Herald* editorial of that date extended congratulations to those who had worked to bring the project to fulfillment:

> They have wrought well, and may the results in good to the community exceed even their fondest expectation.

General Julian S. Carr, Chairman of the Board of Trustees, was "out of town on important business matters and was unable to attend" the opening, noted the newspaper; he did, however, send a letter conveying his best wishes.[2] Mayor J. M. Manning accepted the property for the city, H. L. Carver of the Board of County Commissioners, for the county. The Minutes of the Board of Trustees contained a report describing the new building as being constructed of

> cream tapestry brick with trimmings and columns of old ivory. The broad walk, imposing steps and lovely trees in the yard make a most attractive approach to a Southern library.

The main floor, the report continued, was illuminated by natural light that in combination with the golden oak furniture produced a "restful airy appearance." Along with low tables and chairs,

---

[2]Following the dedication of the new building, General Carr resumed his active support of the institution, acting as Honorary Chairman of the Board of Trustees. At his death in 1924, in accordance with his request, many of his friends gave books to the Library instead of sending flowers to his funeral.

the children's area contained "a lavatory where children who have come in hurriedly from play may wash their hands." The Reading Room had "a fireplace which will add comfort and cheer on cool rainy days." (A balcony was added to the library in 1926; four years later the Children's Room was established in the basement, through the generosity of the Kiwanis Club and after years of impassioned pleas from Miss Crawford.) The new facility had cost $75,000, of which $32,000 was provided by the Carnegie Foundation. While the county's population increased severalfold, this building would remain in use for over fifty years.

So you could enter the Children's Room in the basement without going through the main library on the first floor, your mother turned off Main Street into the driveway and let you out at the outside concrete steps, after which she either drove on back to wait under the trees in the parking lot that held six cars, or else left you to your own happy devices and returned home. The Children's Room held several low tables surrounded by child-sized wooden chairs, together with a circulation desk and card catalogue that were likewise comfortably low; a small magazine section just inside the door contained *Calling All Girls, Nature Magazine, Jack and Jill, The American Girl,* and *Boys' Life;* the walls were lined five feet high with books. A warm and inviting place, the room always had a vaguely pleasant smell all its own — a mixture of old books, new magazines, library paste, wet wool mittens drying on the radiator, and the librarian's English Lavender cologne.

What I read at the library was less remarkable than what I didn't read. In the latter category languished books on radio, stamps, coins, stars, maps, clocks, rocks, trees, rivers, oceans, dinosaurs, wild flowers, birds, snakes, dogs, horses, shells, fish, the human body, electricity, roads, airplanes, autos, government, sports, and science. What remained, though, I read over and over again: the fairy tales — Howard Pyle's *Wonder Clock* and Andrew Lang's *Blue Fairy Book*, Grimm and Andersen, and *Granny's Wonderful Chair;* stories about dolls that could think and talk and sometimes walk, whose owners loved them into life, or who found themselves aboard great sailing ships, or abducted by crows, or rescued by mice; books about children in faraway lands, who wore wooden shoes or silk kimonos and spoke strange languages — Ho-Ming and Little Pear and Young Fu, Nils and Hans Brinker and Heidi; all the Doctor Dolittle stories, and any other books about animals in which the librarian could assure me nothing sad happened — not *Black Beauty* or *Bambi,* naturally, but stories about pet penguins that performed military drills, and a toad that pursued the Life Adventurous, and a small white cat named Good Fortune that received Buddha's own blessing. And there were books about magic amulets, silver bears and Chinese kittens, and books about real children who had enchanted adventures in the heavens, or under the sea, or in the Children's Country; and books about proper English children — Pauline and Petrova and Posy studying ballet, the Bastables seeking treasure and forming a Society for Being Good In, and angelic Sara Crewe, rescued at last from her pinched, miserable existence at Miss Minchin's when her true identity was made known to the wealthy Indian gentleman next door.

The Children's Room had a small but steady group of the faithful who came in to borrow books all year long; but traffic became really brisk early in the summer, when Vacation Reading Club began. Each of us who joined was assigned a construction-paper bookshelf with our name on it, and whenever we finished a book we notified the librarian, who thereupon sat down with us at one of the low tables to query us on the volume's contents. If our answers failed to satisfy her, she would suggest gently but firmly that we take our book back home to review before we again presented ourselves for examination; but if we replied adequately and correctly, she added to our shelf a colored strip of paper on which she'd lettered the book's title. A poster on the bulletin board listed all our names, each one followed by stars indicating how many books that child had read so far — a blue star for each book except for the fifth, which received a silver star, and the tenth, a gold. Vacation Reading Club ended when school started; but in October Mrs. Pridgen arranged a special program during which a librarian first explained to us the importance of reading and then announced the names of Watts Street's Vacation Readers. As she called out names we filed importantly to the front of the auditorium to receive diplomas for participating in the club, together with our book-filled, construction-paper bookcases and an invitation to join again next year.

For seven years I paid my weekly and sometimes semi-weekly visits to the Children's Room, until at twelve I graduated to the adult collection upstairs. (Actually you were supposed to be fourteen before you gained access to the adult area; but after listening to several weeks of pleading, my mother consulted with Miss Crawford, pointing out that I was in the ninth grade and therefore reading on a fourteen-year-old level. After some thought Miss Crawford judiciously decreed that a card might be issued me, but advised my mother to keep an eye on my selection of reading materials, since the library did possess some books that were, as she delicately termed it, Intended For Mature Readers.) Managing the main circulation desk throughout the years I used the library was Miss Sophronia Webb, an attractive but solemn woman who wore horn-rimmed glasses and had short, dark, curly hair. In keeping with the dignity of the library, Miss Webb nearly always wore a correct gabardine or seersucker jacket and skirt with a conservatively ruffled white blouse; and in all the years I saw her we never exchanged a word beyond my murmured "Thank you" after she'd stamped the Date Due slips in my books, and her pleasant but succinct, whispered response, "You're welcome."

For a few weeks after becoming an Adult Reader I drifted uncertainly back and forth between my familiar, well-loved Children's Room and the untried territory of the main floor Young People's Section, until I could get a mental grip on the new area and discover which books there were the good ones. Soon they began to emerge: here were all the Sue Barton books, encompassing vivacious, redhaired Sue's training and entire professional career from *Student Nurse* through *Superintendent of Nurses* to *Visiting Nurse*, including the time she courageously prevented a delirious Spanish patient's escape through a window while she herself was recovering from an emergency appendectomy (the entire hospital staff was awed by her selfless bravery: Dr. Poston himself came in to thank her, and even Miss Cameron, the probationers' stern instructor, offered grudging praise.) Best friends Betsy, Tacy, and Tib grew up together in a world that smelled of roses. Penny Parrish floated happily through a summer of horse shows, military dances, and moonlight picnics; and soon I plunged eagerly into the heady teenage world of proms, taffeta evening dresses, convertibles, joy and heartbreak that resided in *Class Ring* and *Seventeenth Summer*. About the same time I developed a compelling interest in teenage advice books, which advised me to wash out my girdle every night, always to examine the inside seams of a garment before buying it, and not to monopolize the telephone. I also learned that the first and last dances belonged to my escort, that when ordering in a restaurant I must appear uncertain of what I wanted and urge my date to order first (so as to get an idea of how much money he could spend), and that I could draw a silent date into animated conversation by introducing topics that interested him ("Exactly how does the split T formation work, Steve?"). The likelihood of my encountering such taxing social situations seemed remote when the mirror on the wall revealed lank, dishwater-blond hair, nearsighted eyes framed by thick, pink plastic-rimmed glasses, and a figure that possessed all the allure of a board; still, the Ugly Duckling offered some encouragement, and I did read John Robert Powers's "Secrets of Charm" in the *Herald* three times a week. In case a sudden transformation should sweep me into a dizzying whirl of popularity, it was wise to be prepared.

By 10:15 I'd picked out the books I wanted; after Miss Webb had checked them out, I descended the library's stone steps to Main Street and turned right, past the First Presbyterian Church and heading west towards downtown. (To the east was the Trailways station where my mother and I returned from our trips to Raleigh; across from the bus station stood Sears, occupying the spacious building that had been constructed soon after the war.) Across the street from the church stood the Astor Theatre, previously the Ellis, and before that the State, the Russel, and — when it opened in 1935 — the New Theatre: it now showed mostly double features of third-time-returned films. Next to the Astor stood the Durham County Health Department, where my father and I went early each June to get our typhoid shots before swimming season began (my mother was exempt from this duty because once, years before, she had reacted adversely to a typhoid shot and nearly died). On the corner as I crossed Roxboro Street stood the Malbourne Hotel, once "one of the handsomest and best equipped in the South"; since the war, though, the hotel had fallen into the yellow leaf and now catered, rumor had it, to a somewhat irregular clientele.

Just past the Malbourne, and across the street from the YMCA and its splendid neighbor — the County's four-story, Neo-classical Revival Court House — stood the old Orpheum

Theatre, now renamed the Rialto. Half a block west of the theatre, at the corner of Church and Main, I passed The Fashion (Be Sure — It's a Fashion Fashion), which sold the very best lines of women's clothing, and where for years Mrs. Gladys Smoake presided firmly over most of the society weddings in town (favored brides confided proudly, "Mrs. Smoake is doing three weddings on the sixteenth, but she's coming to *ours*").[3] After the Uptown Theatre (formerly the Paramount, and before that the Paris) came one of the more popular downtown restaurants, Harvey's Cafeteria: their food was excellent, but the restaurant was usually crowded by businessmen and women, and I seldom went inside.

A few steps more brought me to the busy corner of Main and Mangum Streets, where I considered Real Downtown began. After checking Walgreen's for new *Captain Marvel*s and *Superman*s, I crossed the street to Kress's and headed straight for the candy counter to review their offerings, which were always the same — silver-wrapped chocolate kisses, sugared orange jelly slices, chocolate wafers covered with white sprinkles, jelly beans, orange-flavored peanuts, and Kernel-Fresh cashews and pecans in heated glass cases. (Holiday seasons did offer additional choices: for Easter, colored candy eggs and chocolate bunnies, yellow marshmallow chicks and rabbits; for Christmas, hard ribbon candy, mellow-cream Santas, and peppermint candy canes.) After standing ritually for a few seconds in front of each case, generally I ended up buying a quarter of a pound of corn candy for ten cents, and then I had something to nibble on while I went back to gaze at the goldfish

[3]A few years later, in 1954, The Fashion's pre-eminence would be challenged by Miss Lillian Montaldo, who opened one of her pink, perfume-scented citadels of feminine elegance only a block north, on the corner of Church and Parrish Streets. Eventually Montaldo's would prove successful; but during its first months the infant store almost foundered, genteel but ignored, until Durham's prominent women discovered it and made it their own.

in their glass tanks. Most of the time I just stood there watching them swim around, but about once a year one of our fish at home died, and then I could buy a replacement. When I'd picked out the liveliest and healthiest-looking one, the salesclerk filled a small, wire-handled, white cardboard carton with water, used a tiny net to capture my fish (managing miraculously to catch the very one I'd chosen, out of the nearly identical dozens that swam in the tank), and deposited him gently inside the carton. Then, of course, I had to take him with me everywhere I went for the rest of the day — to lunch and a movie, as well as on the bus trip home. But it was worth it, I thought, to give him a glass bowl of his very own where he could swim lazily through a towered ceramic castle for entertainment, and have another goldfish for a friend.

From Kress's I went past Butler's Shoes to Baldwin's, The Store of Specialized Shops, which offered gifts, clothing, and a good book department where you could check out the latest fiction for two cents a day. This was a fairly expensive luxury, and only rarely did I take advantage of it; but I did prefer to borrow my racier reading (*Forever Amber* and *Never Love a Stranger*) there rather than at the library, where Miss Webb tended to wrinkle her usually serene brow in a small, worried frown when I brought such titles to the desk. From Baldwin's I jaywalked back across the street to look in the window at Cannon (Red Goose) Shoes before passing Connolly's Jewelers with a quick glance at their silver and china window display; from there I trotted busily on past My Shop's ladies' ready-to-wear, Roscoe Griffin's shoe store, and van Straaten's, to make a quick stop in Silver's 5¢ to $1.00 Store, with its basement grocery where downtown employees frequently shopped after work. (Sometimes I crossed back to inspect the silver patterns in the window of Jones & Frasier, which presented a teaspoon in one's chosen pattern to each girl who graduated from Durham High: it would take me six years to make my choice.)

# Baldwin's Keeps Pace with the Progress of a Great City!

In 1853, R. L. Baldwin's great grandfather had begun the Baldwin tradition with a "general store" up in Buckingham County, Virginia. Down through the years the Baldwin family has kept up this heritage of solid, square-deal principles in merchandising.

Visioning the great future of North Carolina, R. L. Baldwin came to Durham and opened a store. That was in 1911.

Now in 1953, Baldwin's says "Thank You" to all you friends and customers who have contributed to our growth. We are constantly striving to be better—and grow greater with a Great City.

*Foremost in Fashions for Over Forty Years*

*Advertisement in Durham Centennial program, 1953.*

*Advertisement in Durham Centennial program, 1953.*

On to Eckerd Drugs, with its sweet smells of Arpége, Heaven-Sent, and Aquamarine Lotion, and finally my next stop — F. W. Woolworth.

Woolworth's was the best store on the whole block. A sign at the front door, above the tiled "W," urged "Visit Woolworth's Luncheonette"; and usually I did that first, before the crowd rushed in at noon. You could buy a hot dog with cole slaw and chili, with a Coke, for fifteen cents; occasionally, if I were really hungry and had thirty cents, I ordered a hamburger and chocolate milk shake instead. As soon as I could hurry through my lunch and leave my nickel for the waitress, I started purposefully down the aisles to survey the long, waist-high counters filled with merchandise: Tangee Natural and Pink Queen lipsticks, Pond's cold cream, Coty face powder, Maybelline cake mascara; orange and yellow Fiesta Ware, figurines in eighteenth century dress, Aunt Jemima salt and pepper shakers, an assortment of ashtrays (the most popular style had a fire hydrant next to which stood a dog with lifted leg), and vases elaborately decorated with flowers and gold trim,

195

Made in Occupied Japan; endless artificial flowers, jewelry, dresser sets, and hair accessories from snoods to Minnie Mouse plastic barrettes; rows of picture frames containing glamorous photographs of Vivien Leigh, Claudette Colbert, Clark Gable, and Ida Lupino. One whole counter held school supplies: Blue Horse notebooks and paper, Number Two pencils, Esterbrook fountain pens and Skrip ink, and sturdy, belted canvas booksacks in blue, brown, and green.

The toy department offered dolls by the dozen, a few of them black — babies in long gowns, little girls in dimity, an occasional boy doll in cotton sunsuit or corduroy overalls, and — every little girl's dream — the bride dolls in white satin and lace, carefully packaged in boxes with cellophane on top so they could be admired in all their glory without being touched. On a smaller scale, you could buy tiny, two-inch-long pink plastic dolls with movable arms and legs, and a dollhouse full of miniature furniture for them — plastic dining room tables and chairs, wooden radios, refrigerators, and bookcases with books inside. You could find any kind of yoyo you wanted, from elaborately packaged Grand Champions down through more utilitarian and inexpensive models, each one accompanied by instructions for Walking the Dog and going Round the World. There were Mickey Mouse banks and hinged, six-piece wooden "snakes" that convulsively reversed themselves when you folded over the top section; jump ropes, black and white Scottie magnets, and Slinkys; bubble pipes, amber glass piggy banks, and Monopoly sets (Penn Railroad $200). New Golden Books offered stories about Donald Duck and Bugs Bunny, Andy Panda and the Katzenjammer Kids; Big Little Books related Dick Tracy's struggles with mad killers, and Flash Gordon's adventures on Mongo. There were dozens of comics — *Patsy Walker*, the Marvel family, *Superman, Archie, Little Lulu, Looney Tunes and Merrie Melodies* — as well as Betty Grable and Princess Elizabeth paper dolls, Elizabeth Taylor and Carmen

Miranda coloring books. For thirty-nine cents you could buy the inexpensively bound Whitman editions (brown, green, or blue leatherette) that offered classics from *Little Women* to *Treasure Island,* as well as dozens of mystery and adventure stories featuring comic strip characters and movie stars of the day, from *Blondie and Dagwood's Snapshot Clue* to *Judy Garland and the Hoodoo Costume.* And when I was ten, Al Capp's Shmoos appeared; and nearly as soon as those cuddly animals had marched out of the Valley of the Shmoon to offer themselves to mankind,[4] they sprang up in dozens of guises throughout Woolworth's — in books, in plastic replicas of all sizes, and on almost everything else from jewelry to ashtrays, balloons to penny banks.

By now laden with library books and dime store purchases, I left Woolworth's and walked past the dignified, Italianate Fidelity Bank, where I had $14.30 in savings, to turn down

*Fidelity Bank letterhead, ca. 1954.*

Corcoran Street, past the seated group of black women waiting patiently for customers to buy their bright bouquets of zinnias

---

[4]Shmoos were lovable, bewhiskered, ham-shaped white animals, about two feet high. Broiled, their meat tasted like steak; fried, like chicken. They supplied endless amounts of milk, eggs, and butter; their hide made the finest leather (or cloth, depending on how thick you sliced it). Their eyes made splendid suspender buttons; their whiskers, excellent toothpicks. They ate nothing, and multiplied rapidly; if you looked at one hungrily, he dropped dead of sheer joy, but two others immediately appeared to take his place. And if you wanted to have a picnic, you rode the Shmoos to the picnic grounds, ate your fill, and rode the uneaten ones back home.

for fifty cents, and then across the street to look in the windows at Ellis-Stone, Durham's Best Store Since 1886: here were sophisticated mannequins, smartly dressed in well-tailored Handmacher wool suits and holding poodle cloth toppers, or else enveloped in yards of tulle and standing beside a small, discreet sign reading Fascinating Formals, $29.95 And Up. (Ellis-Stone had in 1938 left its former location next to Woolworth's, to occupy the lower floors of the Hill Building, a seventeen-story Art Moderne skyscraper that had replaced the old post office.) From Ellis-Stone I continued down Corcoran to the Washington Duke Hotel where, adopting the dignified mien

*Ellis-Stone in the newly-built Hill Building, ca. 1939.*

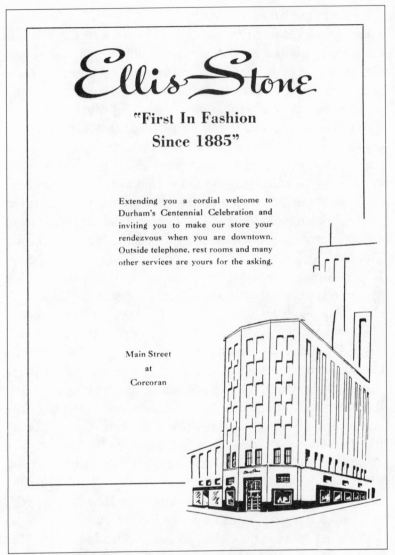
*Advertisement in Durham Centennial program, 1953.*

that I thought suited the hotel's grandeur, I entered through the revolving door, crossed the lobby, and hoped people thought I was a paying guest as I climbed the carpeted stairs to visit the mezzanine ladies' room.

From the Washington Duke I crossed the street to Thomas Book Store, where the saleswomen not only recognized me but also knew I never bought anything, so that I was greeted politely and then left to browse undisturbed. Thomas's offered scrapbooks, diaries, writing paper, greeting cards, and office supplies, together with a gift department that sparkled with crystal vases, music boxes, and porcelain lamps; the hobby and craft section contained Chinese checkers, jigsaw puzzles, and a generous selection of color-coded canvases with which you could paint the picture of your choice, from an anonymous but splendid horse to Da Vinci's "Last Supper." But for me the main attraction was in the rear of the store: aside from the library, Thomas Book Store had the best Young People's Book Department in town. All the series were there (not even the library offered most of these, possibly considering their mass popularity beneath its dignity) — the younger children's books (the Bobbsey Twins, Maida, and Honey Bunch), the clever, cool-headed, courageous sleuths (Nancy Drew, Judy Bolton, and Connie Blair), the dedicated nurses (Sue Barton and Cherry Ames), along with L. M. Montgomery's romantic *Anne* stories, the Betsy-Tacy and Penny Parrish books, and Pollyanna, The Glad Girl. The Doctor Dolittle books were there as well, together with *Janice Meredith, What Katy Did, The Secret Garden* — most of the books I loved, and dozens more I hadn't read. Every week I coveted those books. They were expensive, though — $1.50 each, sometimes more — and always I left with only my library books and my dime store purchases.

But when I was in the eighth grade our school librarian, Miss Whitmore, announced a book contest. A dozen or so of us picked up a sheet of questions about books and authors, looked up the answers, and turned in our entries to be judged. A few days later Miss Whitmore announced that Anne Maxwell had won first prize, a gift certificate worth three dollars at Thomas

Book Store; I had won second, a two-dollar certificate. The following Saturday, prize firmly in hand, I allowed myself an hour to make my choice. Promptly a difficulty arose: what I wanted was not one book, but all of them. Faced with the necessity of limiting my selection, I reluctantly began the painful process of elimination: I'd long since outgrown the Bobbsey Twins and Honey Bunch; all the Betsy-Tacy, Penny Parrish, and Sue Barton books were in the library; my parents gave me Nancy Drews and Judy Boltons for Christmas and birthdays. But the shelves held dozens of others to look at, cherish in hand, and long for; and at last, overcome with frustrated indecision, I strayed desperately into the Adult section, spotted a copy of the store's previous Sunday *Herald* ad listing New Arrivals, and picked up a novel from the list. The book's dust jacket reported that *Raising a Riot* related the hilarious experiences of a man who during his wife's hospitalization had suddenly been forced to keep house, buy groceries, and care for his children. This was clearly an idea to tickle anyone's funnybone, and I was sold. Having made my choice, I took the book and my gift certificate to a saleswoman, who seemed astonished that I was actually making a purchase. Proudly I bore the volume out of the store in a pink-striped Thomas Book Store bag. That evening and the next day I read it through, giggling over the absurdities implicit in the notion of a man's cooking and keeping house; after I'd finished I placed the book carefully in my bookcase, alongside my Nancy Drews. And the next Saturday I was looking yearningly at Thomas's Young People's Books, right on schedule.

Occasionally my routine varied. Once in a while I lunched on chicken chow mein and almond cookies at the Oriental, or else on stuffed peppers and carrot-raisin salad at the Cupboard Cafeteria, which stood conveniently close to Thomas Book Store. Some Saturdays were dental appointment days, and then I nervously took the elevator up to the ninth floor in the Hill

Building to have genial, handsome Dr. Willis clean my teeth or fill a cavity while Miss Parrish held rolls of cotton in my mouth and admonished me gently when the drill hurt and my only recourse was to bite down on her finger. If my mother needed stamps or I had an Overseas Friendship Kit to mail, I went to the columned post office behind the Center Theatre, where I could gaze reverently at the high ceilings, bronze light fixtures, and marble floors as I waited in line at the window. Sometimes I shopped at Belk's, close to Five Points, where I looked at chambray or piqué dresses, or visited the basement to have new rubber taps put on my loafers (keeping my eyes down as I waited, in the hope no one I knew would see me waiting in my stocking feet), or stopped by the shoe department to study my feet in the X-ray machine. (A few years later Belk's would install Durham's first escalator, the store's pride of ownership doubtless dimmed by those of us who persisted in trying to climb the Down escalator when we thought no one was looking.) Rose's 5 & 10 stood across the street from Belk's, and for lunch I could go either to the White Way Lunch in the Piedmont Building, or else around the corner to Amos & Andy, where each day Norris Eubanks served dozens of the best hot dogs in town (occasionally, during rush hours, he entertained his customers by showily lining one arm from shoulder to palm with rolls that he then filled nimbly with hot dogs and condiments, never spilling a drop).

\* \* \* \* \*

Regardless of how I arranged my mornings, Saturday afternoons were for movies, also known as picture shows. Durham had several theaters: the Center (Show Place of Tobaccoland) and the Carolina showed first-run movies; southeast of those two, down on East Main Street, you could catch return engagements at the Uptown, the Criterion, or the Rialto (for a brief time early in the 1950's the Rialto also offered the Hayloft Opry, a live, Saturday night version of what was then disparagingly referred to as "hillbilly" music). Still further east stood the Astor, which after years of showing third-run double features came briefly to life around 1950 to offer such films as *The Red Shoes* and Ingrid Bergman's *Joan of Arc*; there followed a short, unsuccessful incarnation as an art cinema and then a return to double features, this time on the order of *Smashing the Vice Trust* and *Reefer Madness*, while simultaneously questionable-looking individuals took to loitering ominously in front of the building.[5]

Movie times were 1, 3, 5, 7, and 9 p.m. every day except Sunday, when they were 2, 4, and 9 to avoid conflicting with evening services at church. The theaters' newspaper ads seldom bothered to mention starting times, which most people didn't care about anyway: if you arrived a few minutes after the movie had begun, or even during the middle, you just stayed through Pathé News, the previews, and Bugs Bunny until the main feature progressed to where you'd come in. If the film had a particularly surprising conclusion, the theater included a cautionary note in its advertising — "Please! See It From The Beginning!" — and listed the telephone number to call for starting times. To underscore the thematic significance of such movies as *Our Very Own*, which dealt with adoption, or *Pinky* (a black girl passing as white), the ads advised solemnly, "See It With Someone You Love Very Much." In the summertime they also stressed the theaters' air conditioning, which on very hot days was a better drawing card than the films themselves: the Center was The Cool Center (We Manufacture Our Own Weather/Scientifically Air Conditioned), while the Carolina's ads showed the theater's name with icicles hanging from the

---

[5]Wyatt Dixon recalls that in earlier years Durham had other theaters: the Dreamland, the Arcade, the Edisonia, and the Electric (the first to show pictures with sound) were all in existence by 1909; the Grand, the Broadway, and the Strand followed.

letters, or else piled high with frost. The best advertisement of all was a wordless one: when the Carolina's doors were opened, a torrent of cold air rushed vigorously outside, puffing out the triangular flags reading "Cool" that hung from the theater marquee.

Although at one time or another I saw movies at every theater in town, for practical purposes my cinema world consisted of the Center and the Carolina, just a few blocks apart. The Carolina, a slightly aging but still imposing yellow brick building, Beaux Arts in style, had been built by the city in 1926 to provide a replacement facility for the old Academy of Music after the latter had been torn down to make way for the Washington Duke Hotel; originally christened the Durham Auditorium (this name is in fact carved into the marble façade), in 1929 the house was renamed the Carolina Theatre. In addition to its large first-floor auditorium with elevated side boxes, the theater had two balconies, one of them Colored: together the three areas could seat some fourteen hundred persons. The auditorium was designed to present touring stage productions, and during the 1920's and 1930's it offered Durhamites the opportunity to see outstanding actors and actresses starring in some of the most popular plays of the era — Katharine Cornell in *The Barretts of Wimpole Street*, Louis Calhern in *Life With Father*, Katharine Hepburn in *The Philadelphia Story;* but by the time I began going there, the facility had been converted almost entirely to a movie theater with only infrequent stage productions. The Center, on the other hand, was comparatively new, having been built just before World War II; located only a few steps away from the prestigious Washington Duke Hotel and designed exclusively for showing films, it quickly achieved stature as Durham's leading theater.

My visits to Thomas Book Store always ended a few minutes before one o'clock, so I could cross the street to the Center, buy my nine-cent ticket and a Nestlé's Crunch, and hurry inside before the newsreels began. Those were the days when Will Hays and the Motion Picture Production Code reigned,[6] so that parents never worried about what movies a child saw, and I saw them all: the World War II movies with their clean-cut American heroes, bucktoothed Japanese, and bumbling Germans; the Randolph Scott and John Wayne westerns, where Indians and outlaws by the dozens sustained mortal wounds without ever shedding visible blood; the musicals, with Dinah Shore singing "The Last Time I Saw Paris," William Warfield singing "Ol' Man River," and Fred Astaire dancing on the ceiling; the comedies, with Bob Hope zooming through the air, and Abbott and Costello meeting Frankenstein, when they weren't snarling up the French Foreign Legion. A film based vaguely on Annette Kellerman's life had Esther Williams swimming in a huge glass tank, which broke. The charming, dark-haired child of *National Velvet* grew up before our eyes, first in *A Date With Judy* and then in *Conspirator;* and Walt Disney used love-struck centaurs, dancing elephants, and an overconfident mouse to introduce classical music to the provinces. Warmhearted family fare abounded: a Southwestern wife and mother took in a fascinating assortment of boarders to whom she served chicken every Sunday; a pair of efficiency experts efficiently produced a (mostly) neatly regimented brood of twelve children; and a little boy's cherished black ram took Grand Prize at the County Fair. And we cried, and cried — when the already angelic Beth March died, and when an agnostic young country physician returned to Joel McCrea's fold of faith, and when lovable Bobby Driscoll's life was saved by kindly, wise, deep-voiced Uncle Remus.

My mother was always pleased when the Cecil B. DeMille

---

6. . . . when prostitutes were dance-hall girls, every bedroom had twin beds, and even a married couple who found themselves in bed together had to keep one foot on the floor.

Biblical spectaculars came to town, believing their subject matter to be of the uplifting sort that I should be watching instead of so many Bob Hopes and Abbott and Costellos, which she considered harmlessly entertaining but not of lasting value. For my part, I looked forward to such films as *Samson and Delilah* with only slightly less enthusiasm than I had had for *The Paleface*. And rightly so: *Samson and Delilah* had fewer laughs, it was true, but you had the exquisite agony of seeing the red-hot blade come slowly toward you on the screen just as Samson (Victor Mature, meltingly handsome) saw it in the seconds before he was blinded; and then at the very end you had the triumphant exultation of seeing him, his hair grown back and his strength secretly returned, lift his sightless eyes to heaven to pray for help before slowly, methodically pushing against the two large pillars that supported the enormous temple, ignoring the jeers and shouts of the (clearly doomed) heathen crowd, until at last one of the pillars cracked frighteningly and moved ever so slightly, and the throng fell suddenly, dramatically, silent. And then in the hush that followed he continued to push, heaving all his giant strength against the pillars until they gave way and the mighty building collapsed, satisfyingly annihilating all the unbelieving scorners including the temptress Delilah (Hedy Lamarr at her most fetching, in a succession of bare-midriff costumes). DeMille films were always extra long, as befitted the importance of their subject matter, with soaring conclusions that almost invariably left audiences awash in tears. Around the middle, though, you could usually count on some easing of the mood solemn before things became too serious: a banquet scene would be followed by after-dinner entertainment that consisted of scantily-clad, well-endowed young women swaying seductively to M-G-M's notion of Old Testament-era music. (In deference to the Code, however, navels did not show.)

As soon as the Center's movie had ended and the Art Deco

curtain with its hundred eyes had closed firmly over the screen, I collected my books and packages to hurry out of the theater into the blinding sunlight and down Chapel Hill Street to the Carolina, arriving just when the newsreels were beginning for the three o'clock show. Seeing two movies in a row usually provided considerable variety: *Flying Leathernecks* (Marine Air Devils in Hot Pursuit!) with John Wayne at the Center might be followed, for example, by Donald O'Connor and his talking mule at the Carolina. Or Elizabeth Taylor, breathtakingly beautiful in *Father of the Bride,* would precede raucous Marjorie Main in *Ma and Pa Kettle,* or Betty Grable, glamorous as *That Lady in Ermine,* would be followed by artless Ann Blyth in *Mr. Peabody and the Mermaid.* Since movies changed Wednesdays and Sundays, different films played at each theater nearly every Saturday; and it mattered little to me what was showing because I went to see almost anything on the screen, three or four times if I could manage it. But on those rare occasions when the Center was showing a movie I didn't want to see — or else that my mother wouldn't let me see, such as *Stromboli* (Ingrid Bergman's downfall) or *The Yearling* (too sad) — it was easy enough to go straight to the Carolina and watch theirs twice. Movies were better the second time around, anyway.

When the second movie ended it was five o'clock, and time to start home: if it were winter, in fact, the light was already beginning to fade. From the Carolina, lonely and deserted in the late afternoon, I walked up the hill to Chapel Hill Street once more, through Belk's and past United Department Store and Durham Drug to Five Points, where I had to cross two busy streets to get around the hub; but once I did, I could look in the windows of four furniture stores that lined Main Street where the north and westbound buses stopped. Usually I had a few minutes to wait before either the Duke Hospital or Hillsboro Road bus came by, and then there was time to slip into the Tasty Bake Shop, across from the busy Amoco Station,

1853                                    1953

### Forward Durham

WE ARE PROUD TO BE A LINK IN THE
LOCAL COMMERCIAL HISTORY OF THE
CITY OF DURHAM AND TO FURTHER
AID IN THE PROGRESS, GROWTH AND
DEVELOPMENT OF THE COMMUNITY

**E. J. Evans, President**

*Advertisement in Durham Centennial program, 1953.*

for macaroons or a cream horn to take home (by that time my
Kress's corn candy was long gone). And then, depending on
which bus arrived first, I rode past tobacco warehouses, the
Liggett and Myers factory, the Coca-Cola Bottling Plant, and
down Buchanan, past grassy outskirts of the sedately Georgian
Woman's College, once Trinity, and before that — in an earlier,
gayer incarnation — Blackwell's Race Track; or else we went
down Gregson, past the two massive brick buildings that were

# DOWNTOWN

Carr Junior High and Durham High School, staunchly fixed in acreage that early in the century had surrounded playboy Brodie Duke's fine mansion: and off the bus to walk the block to home just as darkness fell.

\* \* \* \* \*

Downtown is different now. Partly that's because my perspective has changed: the blocks I used to walk from east to west have become shorter, and the buildings smaller, than those that inhabit my memory. Mostly, though, the alterations are all too real, caused by the development of shopping centers together with the fact that from the early 1960's until the mid-1970's Urban Renewal swept through Durham with the force of a tidal wave, leaving change and destruction in its wake. Hundreds of businesses, thousands of households were relocated at a cost of millions of dollars; as *Herald* writer Al Wheless summarized the project from his vantage point of 1976, first came the public hearings, then a multi-million dollar bond referendum for public improvements, then planning surveys, and — finally — the bulldozers. Dozens of old landmarks were destroyed; neighborhoods and community ties were disrupted as well, though the planners held that people were moved to "comparable or better" housing. Caught in the throes of one violent change after another, Downtown nearly perished.

The look of Main Street has changed dramatically. The sidewalks have been widened by several feet in order to accommodate new trees and shrubbery, while the street itself has narrowed and become one-way. The library has moved to a large, modern building a block north of its previous columned home (parking spaces are now pleasingly numerous), and some of its former neighbors have played musical chairs: the Sears building now provides space for the Durham County Health Center, while the former Health Department building has become the Department of Social Services Eligibility Office. In

1966 the Malbourne Hotel fell slowly and reluctantly to a wrecking crew that marveled at the old building's toughness; the Durham County Judicial Building now occupies that entire block. The old courthouse that was the backdrop for countless human dramas now stands empty, waiting for imaginative restoration and new life; The Fashion, where so many brides-to-be took their hopes and dreams, has been torn down and replaced by a parking lot. The Montaldo's building still exists, revealing vestiges of its former pink elegance, but the firm itself has long since moved to the large shopping center south of town. Harvey's Cafeteria has disappeared, and the bustling, noisy corner where Walgreen's stood has become a quiet park where weeping willows and crepe myrtles shade concrete benches. Silver's became H.L. Green and then McCrory's, finally closing in 1970; Jones & Frasier left downtown two years later, after spending fifty-five years in one location. The Fidelity Bank was swallowed up by Wachovia, which subsequently moved out of the Geer Building; except for the part housing Woolworth's, that building was destroyed. The site where it stood is now a vacant lot where underground, it is rumored, a fine, costly vault remains and probably will remain forever, for it is much too heavy to be moved at any reasonable expense.

Ellis-Stone, Durham's Best Store Since 1886, exists only under a different name and in another part of town. About a year after William Thalhimer of Richmond came to Durham to become a rice patient, Ellis-Stone was purchased by Thalhimer's, which promptly built a large new store across the street and sold it ten years later to move to a shopping center north of town; Ellis-Stone's former space in the Hill Building is now occupied by the Central Carolina Bank, which has given the building its name. The Belk-Leggett building is gone; across the street the Rose's building stands empty, though the name can still be read on the tiles at the front entrance. The stately Washington Duke Hotel, "the largest and most magnificent in the State," was destroyed in three minutes one December day in 1975, to Durham's disbelieving grief; a parking lot occupies its site, and the discussions that began the next year about the city's need for a downtown hotel continue still. Thomas Book Store closed in 1956; nothing that recalls the store and its array of books, porcelain, and crystal can be seen in the simple, functional realty company building that has replaced it. Five Points, once the city's busy hub as well as the downtown control center and transfer point for the city buses, is now criss-crossed with one-way streets. The Piedmont Building, home of the old White Way Lunch, was torn down in 1966 following a fire; a tranquil, tree-shaded plaza occupies that site. The tetrad of furniture stores, the bake shop, the crowded service station, and the westbound buses have all vanished, leaving no trace.

All but one of the downtown theaters are gone. The Astor closed for the last time in 1954 after nearly twenty years of existence under its various names and identities; the River of Life Gospel Church now occupies (and presumably has sanctified) its site. The Rialto closed in 1970 after fifty-two years of operation, including its first eleven as the Orpheum; during its sunset years, from about 1962 on, it enjoyed a moderately successful renaissance as an art film theater. Around the corner, the Criterion lasted until 1975 after forty-three years in the same location and under the same name, but its building has now disappeared. The Uptown closed in 1965 after a relatively short lifetime, only thirty-seven years. The Center, for some twenty-seven years the leader among downtown theaters, was among the first to go: it vacated its building in 1966, to be quickly replaced by the 1960's-modern Home Savings and Loan building; the street that led down by the side of the theater, where black patrons walked to buy tickets, has been replaced by a park.

But the old Durham Public Library building still stands, the fortunate recipient of loving restoration that whitened the Ionic columns and revealed the lovely yellow brick that had been hidden under white paint for so many years. The First Presbyterian Church continues to watch over its environs, though there's less to watch for now that some former neighbors have vanished from the scene. The Kress Building has been saved, its pinkish-grey marble staircase intact and its façade newly cleaned to reveal beautiful peach, blue, and green terracotta tile decorations that never showed before; with newly darkened windows, the building now houses a number of offices. Viewing the changes in its neighbors with the serenity born of having spent seventy years in one spot, Baldwin's continues to sell women's clothing, although it no longer lends books at two cents a day. Woolworth's likewise continues operations at the site it has occupied since 1915, its exterior sign the same arresting gold letters on carmine red background, the "Visit Woolworth's Luncheonette" signs still in place: the long, waist-high counters, though, have been replaced by floor-to-shoulder shelves; picture frames now enclose either blank orange sheets or photographs of anonymous models; and Mr. T. and Garfield toys have joined the bubble pipes, Monopoly sets, and Slinkys. Both Eckerd's and Durham Drug remain in their old locations, dispensing prescriptions, greeting cards, cosmetics, and health aids, though the latter store now stands stubbornly alone but for one other shop, between a park and a vacant lot. Amos & Andy survives — now on Main Street, across from the old Belk's site, but still offering delicious hot dogs topped with the owner's homemade chili. And the post office stands proudly, its elegance mostly unblemished: the ceiling boasts a fresh coat of paint, red and white geraniums bloom cheerfully in front of the building, and the American flag flies overhead as it has for nearly fifty years.

And in 1978 the Carolina Theatre experienced a miracle, of sorts. Beset by segregation struggles and then by years of declining attendance as the complexion of Downtown changed, the theater that had provided the setting for so many superb stage productions was about to be razed when the Historic Preservation Society came to its rescue by having the building designated a national historic site. A Duke faculty couple who had moved from New York to Durham in 1960, Montrose and Connie Moses,[7] organized a group of friends and supporters into the Carolina Cinema Corporation, a non-profit group dedicated to preserving the theater: they cleaned and scrubbed, scraped and painted until the old building had regained most of her dignity, and subsequently — against the advice of those who warned that "no one will come downtown to movies any more" — redefined the theater's role as that of an art film cinema. As such, the Carolina has successfully supported itself for seven years — has, in fact, taken in well over a million dollars in admission revenues. Now offering the best foreign and art films, the theater shows no signs of losing its appeal: a film distributor has termed it — with the possible exception of one in Miami — the "premier art cinema in the South." And within the past three years the mezzanine lobby has been freed from its dingy, wartime-blacked-window state by Connie Moses and dozens of community supporters, who have transformed

[7] The Moseses' backgrounds are worthy of note. Monte Moses is the son of Dr. Montrose J. Moses, possibly the best-known American drama professor and anthologist of his time. He edited and wrote some forty books, and on his deathbed he instructed his wife that if young Montrose ever showed inclinations toward becoming an actor, he was to be shot. Young Montrose prudently turned his professional interests elsewhere, and became an internationally renowned fine-structure anatomist and cell biologist. His father's theatrical interests survive, though, in his avocations: together with playing a pivotal role in saving and restoring the Carolina, he is a photographer, classical guitarist, and magician.

Connie Moses, who died in April of 1985, was an accomplished dressmaker and milliner, an expert costume historian, and a gifted actress and singer. The ballroom into which she breathed new life became her special pride, and provided the setting for her last concert, four weeks before her death.

the room into a stunning rose and burgundy fantasy complete with velvet sofas and curtains, ostrich feathers, and colorful, three-dimensional theater memorabilia — a matador's costume, a fluffy tutu, a violin and bow — in frames that decorate the walls. The room, which the City has christened the Connie Moses Ballroom, now provides the setting for gatherings of the Friends of the Carolina, community meetings, private parties, and Sunday afternoon musicales. Vision, hard work, and determination have been rewarded: the Carolina thrives.

*Durham City and all it ever was, is, or will be,*
*is a direct product of tobacco.*
*It eats, breathes, sleeps and has its being*
*in tobacco and woe be the day should we lose*
*the tobacco business, or any citizen lay his hand*
*upon it in any way to throttle it.*

*— Zalph A. Rochelle, 1953*

# Epilogue

Together with the visual alterations to Downtown, Durham itself has changed. Tobacco and textiles, once the city's undisputed industrial giants, have been greatly weakened: while textiles suffer from foreign imports, the tobacco industry reels from blows inflicted by everyone from the American Cancer Society to the Surgeon General. Duke University, established and supported by tobacco money, now sponsors a Quit Smoking clinic, while a short distance away stands a bronze statue of the school's founder, cigar in hand, presumably viewing such sacrilege in patient forbearance. Durham newspapers maintain an uneasy balance between proliferating evidence of tobacco-linked health problems (which, to their credit, they report faithfully and fully), and an anguished awareness of tobacco's economic importance to their town and to the state. Caught on the horns of a painful dilemma, the city seems to be pinning its hopes on high-tech industry: nearby the Research Triangle Park, already twenty-five years old, houses chemical, electronics, computer, and software companies among its dozens of firms. North of town, meanwhile, three historic plantation lands totaling over five thousand acres are to undergo commercial and residential development, the nature — and impact — of which as yet remain unknown.

In 1884 Durham's first historian wrote poetically of having viewed

> this busy little city — a town that in sixteen years or less has grown from nothing to be a busy and prosperous city of over 5,000 inhabitants. In every direction could be heard the hum and buzz of machinery, mingled with the song of the saw, and the sound of the hammer. Heavily loaded wagons and drays rattled over the newly-made, rock-paved streets. Magnificent buildings lined each side of the way, elegant dwellings could be seen in the distance, churches with their tall spires almost kissing the clouds stood here and there, factory bells and steam whistles sent forth their evening signals. Everything is hurry and bustle. Progress and enterprise is evident on every side, and to think that where this proud and famous little city now stands was, a few years ago, almost a wilderness. Is it not a grand illustration of what enterprise and energy can do?

By 1925 William Kenneth Boyd spoke approvingly not only of the town's spirit of work and its steady expansion of business and industry, but also its harmonious race relations, individualism, and increasing cooperation in causes related to public welfare. Twenty-five years later, when tobacco and textiles still ruled, W. C. Dula wrote,

> The death of the Confederacy gave birth to the city of Durham, and out of the ashes of the hopes of the Southern people has been built a great and progressive city.

Who will speak for Durham next, and what message will he bring?

March, 1986

# NOTES

ABBREVIATIONS USED IN NOTES

DDS        *Durham Daily Sun*
DMH        *Durham Morning Herald*
DS         *Durham Sun*
Minutes, DPL  *Minutes of the Board of Trustees, Durham Public Library*
MH         *Morning Herald*
TFC        *This Fabulous Century*
TC         *Time Capsule*

Prologue.

This brief summary of Durham's early history is based primarily on William Kenneth Boyd's *Story of Durham* (1925), which, though attentive to detail, unfortunately contains neither bibliography nor notes. In addition, Hiram Paul's *History of Durham* (1884) is invaluable for a detailed account of the town's beginnings and first twenty years, as well as for contemporary character sketches of General Julian S. Carr, William T. Blackwell, Washington Duke, and others. W. C. Dula's *Durham and Her People* (1951) relies on Paul and Boyd for most of the town's early history, but adds an interesting potpourri of information about individuals and business firms. A good account of Pinhook can be found in George Lougee's "Durham of Yesteryear: Rowdy and Roaring," DMH 4 Feb 1976. Robert F. Durden's *Dukes of Durham* (1975) offers a detailed, solidly researched, and thoroughly fascinating account of the Dukes' business activities (Benjamin Duke is here, for the first time, given his due) as well as of the family's relations with Trinity College and Durham.

For a lighter approach to Durham's early history, see Frances Gray Patton's "The Town Bull Durham Built," *Holiday*, 26 (December, 1959), p. 96.

Specific references follow:

5-6   The episode of the Union and Confederate armies' sacking John Green's store of tobacco is described at length in Paul, pp. 25-26.

6-7   Comments about W. T. Blackwell are in Paul, p. 131.

8-9   "a high-living...sporting town" and other observations in this paragraph are from Dula, pp. 10-11.

8n.   Washington Duke's comment about his son is quoted in Jonathan Daniels's *Tar Heels: A Portrait of North Carolina* (1947), p. 111.

219

# HEAVEN FOR BEGINNERS

One: Parents First.

15    Historical background on Hillsborough is excerpted from Lucile Noell Dula, *Pelican Guide to Hillsborough* (1979), pp. 15-18.

15-17    Details of the family's farm life and of my father's early years in Durham were supplied by S. A. McBroom.

18    Details of the ending of trolley service in Durham came from DMH 26 Jan, 31 Jan, 1 Feb, 2 Feb 1930, and from S. A. McBroom.

21-23    Details of my mother's family background and childhood are taken from her book, *An Orange County Childhood* (1983).

23    Septic tanks in West Durham, MH 14 Jul 1917.

23-24    Facts on Durham and its industry in 1917 are taken from that year's *City Directory.*

24-34    Information about downtown commercial establishments, theaters, and their offerings came primarily from ads in the MH of June and July, 1917, and from the 1917 *City Directory.*

26-27    Fraternity pledge activities' details were supplied by S. A. McBroom.

29    First Presbyterian Church construction, in Boyd, p. 194.

29-30    Destruction of Carrolina, in Dula, p. 15.

30    Courthouse opening, MH 27 Nov 1916.

30-32    Orpheum opening, MH 29 Nov 1916.

32-33    *Birth of a Nation,* in Wyatt Dixon, "How Times Do Change," DS 11 May 1979.

32-33    Academy of Music offering advertised in MH 9 Sep 1917.

33    Gosden/Correll meeting described by Wyatt Dixon, DS 17 Nov 1972.

33    Hotel Lochmoor dance lessons advertised in MH 10 Jul 1917.

34-35    Music schools described and advertised in MH 2 Sep 1917, and in the *City Directory.*

35    Southern Conservatory of Music described by Wyatt Dixon, DS 19 Mar 1976.

35    Violano Virtuoso advertised in MH 17 Jun 1917.

35-37    National Religious Training School described by Wyatt Dixon, DS 4 Oct 1985.

37    Trinity College statistics in *City Directory,* 1917.

37    Trinity graduation account in MH 6 Jun 1917.

37    Trinity vegetable garden described in MH 8 Jul 1917.

39    Katie L. Johnson's photographs advertised, MH 9 Sep 1917.

39    Durham Book and Stationery's ad for gold-stamped Bibles, MH 28 Jul 1917.

39    Lakewood Park Shooting Gallery advertised, MH 21 Jun 1917.

40-41    Information about the Class of 1925 is taken from Ruth G. McBroom's (homemade) yearbook.

40-41    May Day exercises described in DMH 8 May 1925.

41    "one in which profound thought was shown..." DMH 1 Jun 1925.

42    Information on George Watts's arrival in Durham and partnership in W. Duke, Sons and Co. comes from Durden, p. 18.

42    "one of our most worthy..." in Paul, p. 85.

42    Founding of Home Savings Bank, Durham Loan and Trust, YMCA, and construction of new First Presbyterian Church in Boyd, pp. 119, 267, 194; Durden, p. 148.

# NOTES

42     "Of his riches...." Boyd, pp. 194-95.
42-45   History of Watts Hospital is excerpted from Boyd, pp. 211-18.
43     "It has been my desire...." quoted in Boyd, p. 213.
43     "It is appropriate...." quoted in Boyd, p. 214.
44-45   "May it ever be conducted...." quoted in Boyd, p. 218.
45-46   Information about Watts Hospital in 1927 comes from Ruth G. McBroom.
49     Taxpayers League information in George Lougee, "With Nation in Deathlock, Taxpayer's League Formed a Posse," DMH 22 Jul 1984.


Three: Pleasures Free

77-80   This account of Lakewood Park has been compiled primarily from Charles Barbour's "Lakewood Park...Remember?", DMH 16 Sep 1962; Claudia P. Roberts's *Durham Architectural and Historical Inventory* (1982), pp. 245-46; Wyatt Dixon's "Story of Recreation," DS 21 Oct 1983; George Lougee's "He Has Memories of Lakewood Park," DMH 24 Dec 1978; and the recollections of S. A. McBroom and Ruth G. McBroom. Specific references follow.
77     "It was the first time...." MH 4 Jul 1902.
77     "Lakewood is the name...." DDS 7 Jul 1902.
77     Gala opening date is from Wyatt Dixon, DS 21 Oct 1983.
78     "agreeably rendered" in MH 15 Jun 1903.
78     Draining of mud-bottomed pool is described by George Lougee, DMH 24 Dec 1978.
78     "City Water, etc." advertised in DMH 31 May 1925.
78     Story of absent-minded businessman is told by Wyatt Dixon, DS 21 Oct 1983.
79     Admission costs, High Class shows advertised in DDS 3 Jun 1912.
79     Request for waterfront room in Wyatt Dixon, DS 21 Oct 1983.
79     Razzle-Dazzle popcorn mentioned by George Lougee, DMH 24 Dec 1978.
79     Zoo animals, Electric Studio advertised in MH 17 Jun 1917.
79     Diving for silver coins advertised in MH 11 Jul 1917.
80-83   Parts of this account of the Children's Museum were taken from undated newspaper articles in the Museum's scrapbooks. Specific references follow.
80     Hornaday Foundation support, in DMH 24 Mar 1946.
81     Meadow Brook Saddle Club show, in DMH 9 Jun and 22 Jun 1947.
81     Kiwanis Club support, in DMH 18 Jul 1947.
81     Move to Hillandale, DMH 2 Nov 1947.
81     Move to Murray Avenue, DMH 10 Dec 1962.
88     Historical background on *Amos 'n' Andy* is from *All About Amos 'n' Andy And Their Creators, Correll and Gosden* (1929), pp. 36-43.
88-89   Nation's interest in *Amos 'n' Andy* described in John Dunning, *Tune In Yesterday* (1976), p. 33.
89     Shaw quoted in Dunning, p. 36.
93-94   "Twenty-five cents per room, per week" — this information supplied by Vallie Robinson.

# HEAVEN FOR BEGINNERS

100-01    Details of Duke Park's opening are from DMH 2 Aug 1934; Mrs. Stelling's comment appeared in DMH 3 Aug 1934.

104    Details of water pageant from DMH 12 Aug 1949.


## Four: Knowledge Curious

109-11    Information on Mrs. Vera Twaddell has been compiled primarily from George Lougee's "She's Taught Music To Three Generations," DMH 22 Aug 1975; the Trinity College yearbook for 1920; and a personal interview, 5 Apr 1984.

110    Durham Children's Choir School, DMH 22 Mar 1925.

110    "The community choir will perhaps...." DS 23 Mar 1925.

111    State choral contest in DS 20 Jun 1947.

111    Death of W. P. Twaddell in DMH 16 Aug 1949.

111    "dominated choral music...." DMH 18 Aug 1949.

114-15    This account of Watts Street School has been compiled partly from an undated copy of a DMH article supplied by the Durham City Schools office. The faculty listing indicates that the article was published prior to 1945.

114    "The equipment of...." MH 1 Oct 1916.

114    "The playground is...." MH 8 Oct 1916.

114    Grade totals in 1923 came from a published *Report of the Superintendent, Durham City Schools, 1914-1923* (1923), p. 37.

115    "In recognition of...." DMH 2 Feb 1929.

115-17    Information on Mrs. Lorraine Pridgen has been compiled from Suzanne Jones, "From Books To Bread-Making Will Be The Change For Retiring Educator, Mrs. Lorraine Pridgen," DMH 4 May 1962, and from a personal interview, 30 Jun 1984.

124    "Miss Dove was a certainty...." Frances Gray Patton, *Good Morning, Miss Dove* (1954), p. 8.

124    "She had an extra quality...." Patton, p. 21.

124    "Her love flowed out...." Patton, p. 139.

124    "Each June some forty-odd little girls and boys...." Frances Gray Patton, "The *Terrible* Miss Dove," in *Twenty-Eight Stories* (1969), p. 117.


## Five: Dreams, Books

130-32    Several examples of Nancy's physical and mental prowess have been borrowed from Arthur Prager, "The Secret of Nancy Drew," *Saturday Review of Literature*, 25 Jan 1969, pp. 18-19, 34-35.

131    "a constant stream of good-natured banter" — in Carolyn Keene, *The Clue in the Diary* (1932), pp. 72-73.

131    "completely lacking in good manners" — in Carolyn Keene, *The Hidden Staircase* (1959), p. 38.

132    "had never seen a negro...." in Margaret Sutton, *The Haunted Attic* (1932), p. 35.

133-34    Ads from *Patsy Walker*, No. 51 (March, 1954).

# NOTES

Six: Stars in My Crown

145-48 Historical background on Asbury Church comes from the church's history, *The Asbury Trail* (1972), and from Wyatt Dixon, DS 8 Mar 1974.
146-47 Church's opening services described in DMH 15 Aug 1927.
147-48 Mortgage payments listed in church bulletin, 14 Dec 1941.
155 "This church building will never stand...." My thanks to Gladys Bunting for this story.
159n. For a detailed account of the Dukes' support of Methodism, see Durden.
160 Weston LaBarre's *They Shall Take Up Serpents: Psychology of the Southern Snake-Handling Cult* (1962) provides a thorough study of this unusual phenomenon.


Seven: Praise The Lord And Pass The Ammunition

165-71 For background information on World War II's home front, I have relied heavily on the *Time Capsules* for 1941 through 1945 (New York: Time-Life Books, 1967 and 1968), and on *This Fabulous Century*, Vol. 5: 1940-50 (New York: Time-Life Books, 1969). Specific references follow:
166 The metal salvage cartoon appeared in *The New Yorker War Album* (1942).
166 Science museums' precautions are from *Time Capsule* 1942 (1968), pp. 174-75.
167 Conversion of liquor companies is from TC 1942, p. 191.
167 Cartoon characters' war activities are from *This Fabulous Century*, Vol. 5: 1940-50 (1969), pp. 180-83.
167 Disappearance of sage and saffron, TC 1941, p. 206.
167-68 Disappearance of desserts at White House, TC 1942, p. 13.
168 Twentieth-Century-Fox cuts banquet scenes, TC 1943, p. 24.
168 King George VI's wartime measures, TC 1942, p. 153.
168 Tallulah Bankhead's offer, TC 1942, p. 153.
168 Carole Lombard's death, TC 1942, pp. 20-21.
168-69 Bing Crosby's "White Christmas," TC 1942, p. 166.
169 Sonja Henie's insurance application, TC 1943, p. 130.
169 Jimmy Stewart's service, TC 1944, p. 189.
169 Bob Hope's entertaining troops, TC 1943, pp. 141-42.
169 Increase in sales of books with religious themes, TC 1943, p. 175.
169 Congressional Medal of Honor award, TC 1945, pp. 222-23.
169 Karl Barth comment, TC 1941, p. 188.
169 Pearl Harbor chaplain, TC 1942, p. 69.
169-70 Women as war workers, TC 1942, pp. 30-31.
170 Albina pledge, TC 1943, p. 190.
170-71 Fashion's military air, TFC 1940-50, pp. 254-55.
171 Wartime regulations for civilian garments, TFC 1940-50, p. 248.
171 *Vogue* choices, TFC 1940-50, p. 248.
171-72 "What should have been a great occasion...." is from Hersey Everett Spence, *I Remember* (1954), p. 181.
172 Malbourne Hotel on weekends, in George Lougee, "Malbourne Drew GIs, Elite," DMH 24 Jun 1984.

173   Flag offer in DS 26 May 1942.
174   Ernie Pyle on Normandy, in DMH 17 Jun 1944.
175   Instructions on stamp values quoted in TFC 1940-50, p. 164.
178   Rockefeller Plaza celebration, TC 1944, pp. 33-34.
179   Lights on in Paris, TC 1945, p. 131.
179   Eisenhower welcome, TC 1945, pp. 85-86, 55.
179   Sailor kiss, TFC 1940-50, p. 211.
179   War Production Board, TC 1945, pp. 55-56.
179   Excess war supplies, TC 1945, p. 56.
179   Bars of Manhattan, TC 1945, p. 57.

Eight: Downtown

183-87   Historical background on the library comes partially from Betty Irene Young, "Lillian Baker Griggs: Pioneer Librarian," *The Durham Record* (1983), pp. 26-36, and from Boyd, pp. 262-66. Other specific references follow:
184   "The day has arrived...." DDS 10 Feb 1898.
184   "The building is a beauty...." and details of opening reception are in DDS 11 Feb 1898.
185n.   "...our regret at her resignation...." *Minutes of the Board of Trustees, Durham Public Library,* meeting of 6 Nov 1923.
186   Mrs. Griggs at Lochmoor, in Young, pp. 35-36.
186   "They have wrought well...." is in DMH 6 Jul 1921.
186   Opening, Carr absence are in DMH 7 Jul 1921.
186n.   Carr's death in Boyd, p. 265.
186-87   "cream tapestry brick...." and other descriptions are in typed report in *Minutes, DPL.*
187   Addition of balcony and Children's Room are in *Minutes, DPL.*
191   "one of the handsomest...." quoted by George Lougee, "Malbourne Drew GIs, Elite," DMH 24 Jun 1984.
197n.   Information on the characteristics of Shmoos is excerpted from Al Capp, *The Life and Times of the Shmoo* (1949).
202-03   Hayloft Opry was advertised in DMH 5 Jul 1951.
203n.   Early theaters were discussed by Wyatt Dixon, DS 11 May 1979.
208-09   Brodie Duke's home was pictured and briefly described in Joel A. Kostyu and Frank A. Kostyu, *Durham: A Pictorial History* (1978), p. 130.
209   Urban Renewal was discussed in Al Wheless's article, DMH 9 Aug 1976.
209-10   Destruction of Malbourne was described by George Lougee, DMH 24 Jun 1984.
211   Burning of Piedmont Building was mentioned by Wyatt Dixon, DS 29 Feb 1976.
211   Closing dates and previous names of downtown theaters and commercial establishments have been collected primarily from Durham's *City Directories.*
212-14   Information on Carolina Theatre comes from Kim Devins, "To Durham With Love," *Spectator* (1984), pp. 37-40, and from personal interviews with Monte and Connie Moses.

# NOTES

Epilogue.

217 The Quit Smoking Clinic is described in *Duke: A Magazine for Alumni and Friends, 72,* 3 (Jan/Feb 1986), pp. 36-37.

218 "this busy little city...." — Paul, pp. xvi-xvii.

218 Boyd's comments are on pp. 322-25.

218 "The death of the Confederacy...." — Dula, p. 1.

# BIBLIOGRAPHY

## ANNOTATED LIST OF WORKS CITED

*All About Amos 'n' Andy and Their Creators Correll and Gosden.* New York: Rand McNally, 1929.
An informal, simply-written account of how Correll and Gosden met and developed their show.

*The Asbury Trail: A brief history of the Asbury United Methodist Church, Durham, N.C. 1893-1971.*

Boyd, William Kenneth. *The Story of Durham, City of the New South.* Durham: Duke University Press, 1925.
Attentive to detail and warm toward its subject matter, but unfortunately lacking in notes and bibliography.

Capp, Al. *The Life and Times of the Shmoo.* New York: Pocket Books, 1949.
The authoritative study.

Devins, Kim. "To Durham With Love." *Spectator* (30 Aug 1984), pp. 37-40.
A good account of the Carolina Theatre Ballroom's restoration.

Dixon, Wyatt. Numerous articles, individually cited in Notes.

Dunning, John. *Tune In Yesterday.* Englewood Cliffs, N.J.: Prentice Hall, 1976.
Excellent summaries of programs from radio's Golden Age.

Dula, Lucile Noell. *The Pelican Guide to Hillsborough: Historic Orange County, North Carolina.* Gretna, La.: Pelican Publishing Co., 1979.
A well-illustrated introduction to Hillsborough, with emphasis on the town's historic houses.

Dula, W. C. *Durham and Her People.* Durham: The Citizens Press, 1951.
An unusual and interesting potpourri of information about businesses and individuals of Durham — some well-known, some not.

Durden, Robert F. *The Dukes of Durham, 1865-1929.* Durham: Duke University Press, 1975.
A detailed study of the Dukes and their business activities. Solidly researched, fascinating reading.

*Durham, North Carolina: A Center of Industry and Education.* Durham Chamber of Commerce, 1926.
Proud panoply of Durham's offerings.

Keene, Carolyn. *The Clue in the Diary.* New York: Grosset & Dunlap, 1932.

————. *The Hidden Staircase.* New York: Grosset & Dunlap, 1959.

Kostyu, Joel A. and Frank A. Kostyu. *Durham: A Pictorial History.* Norfolk: The Donning Company, 1978.
Splendid collection of old photographic views, with brief but informative supporting text.

LaBarre, Weston. *They Shall Take Up Serpents: Psychology of the Southern Snake-Handling Cult.* Minneapolis: University of Minnesota Press, 1962.
Careful sociological and psychological study of an unusual religious group.

Lougee, George. Numerous articles, individually cited in Notes.

McBroom, Ruth Gates. *An Orange County Childhood.* Orlando, 1983.

*Minutes of the Board of Trustees, Durham Public Library.*

*Patsy Walker.* (No. 51, March, 1954.) New York: Bard Publishing, 1953.

Patton, Frances Gray. *Good Morning, Miss Dove.* New York: Dodd, Mead, 1954.
A delightful classic.

————. "The Town Bull Durham Built." In *Holiday, 26* (December, 1959), p. 96.
Lighthearted account of Durham's beginnings.

————. *Twenty-Eight Stories.* New York: Dodd, Mead, 1969.
Subtle, sensitive, and witty.

Paul, Hiram. *History of the Town of Durham, N.C.* Raleigh: Edwards, Broughton, 1884.
Includes a detailed account of the town's beginnings and first twenty years, as well as contemporary character sketches of General Julian S. Carr, William T. Blackwell, Washington Duke, and others. Has a number of interesting ads for Durham's early businesses.

Prager, Arthur. "The Secret of Nancy Drew." *Saturday Review of Literature* (25 Jan 1969), pp. 18-19, 34-35.

Pridgen, Lorraine Iseley. Personal interview. 30 Jun 1984.

Roberts, Claudia P., *et al. The Durham Architectural and Historic Inventory.* City of Durham, North Carolina, 1982.
Excellent historical studies of Durham neighborhoods and commercial districts. Generously illustrated.

Spence, Hersey Everett. *"I Remember": Recollections and Reminiscences of Alma Mater.* Durham: The Seeman Printery, 1954.
Enjoyable, occasionally crochety recollections of Trinity and Duke, covering the period 1903-1952.

Sutton, Margaret. *The Haunted Attic.* New York: Grosset & Dunlap, 1932.

*This Fabulous Century, Vol. 5: 1940-50.* New York: Time-Life Books, 1969.
Good informal history of the 1940's.

# BIBLIOGRAPHY

*Time Capsule/1941.* New York: Time-Life Books, 1967.
*Time Capsule/1942.* New York: Time-Life Books, 1968.
*Time Capsule/1943.* New York: Time-Life Books, 1968.
*Time Capsule/1944.* New York: Time-Life Books, 1967.
*Time Capsule/1945.* New York: Time-Life Books, 1968.
Excerpts from *Time* magazines for the years indicated.

Twaddell, Vera Carr. Personal interview. 5 Apr 1984.

Young, Betty Irene. "Lillian Baker Griggs: Pioneer Librarian." In *The Durham Record,* 1 (Fall, 1983), pp. 26-52.
A detailed and readable account of Mrs. Griggs's career at the Durham Public Library and at Duke. Careful notes.


## OTHER PRINTED SOURCES

*Durham City Directory.*
*Durham Daily Sun.*
*Durham Morning Herald.*
*Durham Sun.*
*Morning Herald.*


## ALSO RECOMMENDED

Andrews, R. McCants. *John Merrick: A Biographical Sketch.* Durham: Seeman Printery, 1920.
Reverential biography of one of the founders of N.C. Mutual Life Insurance Co.

Bevington, Helen. *Along Came the Witch: A Journal in the 1960's.* New York: Harcourt Brace Jovanovich, 1976.

—————. *Beautiful Lofty People.* New York: Harcourt Brace Jovanovich, 1974.

—————. *A Book and a Love Affair.* New York: Harcourt Brace & World, 1968.

—————. *The House was Quiet and the World was Calm.* New York: Harcourt Brace Jovanovich, 1971.

—————. *The journey is everything: a journal of the Seventies.* Durham: Duke University Press, 1983.

—————. *When Found, Make a Verse of.* New York: Simon and Schuster, 1961.
Charming, witty works — verse, essays, journals, a commonplace book — by a Professor of English at Duke.

Biddle, Cordelia Drexel. *My Philadelphia Father.* Garden City: Doubleday, 1955.
Biography of the colorful Anthony J. Drexel Biddle by his daughter, who married Angier B. Duke. Some amusing observations on the Dukes and Durham.

229

# HEAVEN FOR BEGINNERS

Chaffin, Nora Campbell. *Trinity College, 1839-1892: The Beginnings of Duke University.* Durham: Duke University Press, 1950.
Meticulous history of Trinity from its beginnings as Brown's Schoolhouse, until its move to Durham.

Daniels, Jonathan. *Tar Heels: A Portrait of North Carolina.* New York: Dodd, Mead & Company, 1947.
Interesting chapters on tobacco, the Dukes, North Carolina Mutual (from a 1947 viewpoint).

Evans, Eli N. *The Provincials: A Personal History of Jews in the South.* New York: Atheneum, 1973.
Evans's recollections of his Durham boyhood, skillfully interwoven with numerous interviews and careful research.

Jenkins, John Wilber. *James B. Duke: Master Builder.* New York: George H. Doran Company, 1927; rpt. Spartanburg, S.C.: The Reprint Co., 1971.
Homage-filled; no bibliography or notes.

Mebane, Mary. *Mary.* New York: Viking Press, 1981.
Moving account of growing up black in Durham during the 1930's and 1940's.

Murray, Pauli. *Proud Shoes: The Story of an American Family.* New York: Harper & Row, 1978.
A fascinating and meticulous account of several generations of a (free) mixed-race family. The author grew up next to Durham's Maplewood Cemetery; a lawyer, she later became the first black woman to be ordained an Episcopal priest.

Porter, Earl W. *Trinity and Duke 1892-1924: Foundations of Duke University.* Durham: Duke University Press, 1964.
Detailed history of Trinity from the time of its move to Durham, until its transformation into Duke University.

Sanders, Charles Richard. *The Cameron Plantation in Central North Carolina (1776-1973) and Its Founder Richard Bennehan.* Durham: C. R. Sanders, 1974.
Warm, sensitive historical account of the Cameron Plantation. Generously illustrated, with helpful map.

Seeman, Ernest. *American Gold.* New York: Dial Press, 1978.
A sprawling, untidy, raucous novel, sometimes entertaining. Local history buffs may enjoy identifying events and characters of Durham's past. Author was a member of the family that for many years owned and operated Seeman Printery; for a time he headed the Duke University Press.

Winkler, John F. *Tobacco Tycoon: The Story of James Buchanan Duke.* New York: Random House, 1942.
A sensational, sometimes melodramatic account. No bibliography or notes.

# INDEX

*(Illustrations in Italics)*

# INDEX

# INDEX

W. Duke, Sons and Company, 7-8, *24*
Wake County, 9
Walgreen's, 192, 210
Wall, Marjorie, 111
Wallace the Magician, 134
Warren, Billy, 66
Washington Duke Hotel, 47-48, *48*,
   100, 198-200, 204, 210-11
Watts, George Washington, 42-45,
   115
*Watts Hi-Lights,* 117
Watts Hospital, 94
   original facility donated by G. W.
      Watts (1895), 42-43, *44*
   community's support for, 43-44
   second facility donated by Watts
      (1909), 44-45, *45*
   in 1927, 45-46
Watts Street Grocery, 94
Watts Street School; *see* George Watts
   School
WDNC, 82
WDUK, 82
Webb, Sophronia, 189-90
Wells Dramatic Company, 78
West Durham Methodist Church, 19
   *see also* Asbury Methodist Church
West Durham School, 39, 40-41
   Class of 1925 graduation exercises, 41
Wheless, Al, 209
White Way Lunch, 202, 211
Whitmore, Sadie, 200
Williams, Jean, 114
Willis, Guy, D.D.S., 201-02
Wilson, Jane, 120
"Womanless Weddings," 157
Woman's College (Duke University),
   53, 152, 208
Woolworth, F. W., 25, 210, 212
   during the 1940's, 195-97
World War II
   saving, conservation, and shortages,
      165-68
   contributions by the famous, 168-69
   religion in, 169
   women in, 169-70
   fashions during, 170-71
   in Durham, 171-72
   newspapers during, 173-74
   rationing during, 173, 175
   end of, 178-79
Wright, Richard H., 77
Wright's Grocery, 39

Wynn, Mrs. A. R., 35
Wynne, George V., 27

YMCA, 30, *31*

"Zesto," 95
Zion Tabernacle, 160
Zollicoffer, Mary J., 120